BENEVON.
BEYOND
THE ASK EVENT
FULLY INTEGRATING THE BENEVON MODEL

TERRY AXELROD

Beyond the Ask Event—Fully Integrating the Benevon Model
Terry Axelrod

Benevon (formerly Raising More Money) Publications,
Seattle, Washington
The following trademarks appear throughout this book:
Benevon™, Treasure Map®, Point of Entry®, Next Step®,
Free Feel-Good Cultivation Event™, Cultivation Superhighway™,
Ask Event™, Essential Story™, Visionary Leader™,
Emotional Hook™, Know-Thy-Donor Program™,
Multiple-Year Giving Society™, Passion Retread™,
Units of Service™, Five-Step Follow-Up Call™.

For information, please contact:
Benevon Publications, 2100 North Pacific Street, Seattle, WA 98103

Although the author and publisher have made every effort
to ensure the accuracy and completeness of information
contained in this book, we assume no responsibility
for errors, inaccuracies, omissions, or any inconsistencies herein.
Any slights of people, places, or organizations are unintentional.

First edition published in 2007.

ISBN: 978-0-9700455-7-7

The Library of Congress Cataloging-in-Publication Data
is available from the publisher.

ATTENTION CORPORATIONS, UNIVERSITIES,
COLLEGES, AND PROFESSIONAL ORGANIZATIONS:
Quantity discounts are available on bulk purchases of this book
for educational purposes. Special books or book excerpts can also be
created to fit specific needs. For information, please contact:
Benevon Publications, 2100 North Pacific Street, Seattle, WA 98103
Phone 888-322-9357

ACKNOWLEDGMENTS

Thanks to our alumni organizations, especially those who are part of our Sustainable Funding Program, for allowing us to work with you to develop and test the material presented in this book. Theories and models are only useful if they can be widely adapted and customized. Without your willingness to "pilot" many of these strategies, this book would not have been possible.

Next, thanks to our instructors, coaches, and staff, especially to Lynda Bowman, Tammy Zonker, Sharon Ervine, and Linda Ray, who share my obsession with having each of our groups be successful in attaining its own definition of sustainable funding. Without that passion for having the work of each nonprofit be known and fulfilled in the world, this process would be hollow. With it, the work of evolving the model has been exciting and rich.

To the "village" of people it has taken to produce this book, I offer sincere thanks, especially to Ann Overton, Elizabeth Smith, Paulette Eickman, Miriam Lisco, Lisa McCune, and Virginia See for the unique contribution each of them has made to what you are about to read. Their generous spirit and teamwork exemplify the principles of the model and have kept the process upbeat and fun.

Finally, my deepest gratitude to Suzanne Shoemaker, Stephanie Nelson, and Alan Axelrod, who make it all work.

TABLE OF CONTENTS

Appendix

PREFACE

Ever since our first Benevon (formerly Raising More Money) 101 Workshop in 1996, I have been saying the same thing every day: sustainable funding, sustainable funding, sustainable funding. But when spoken into a world of scarcity, what people hear is: short-term fix, quick money, and basic survival. Long-term sustainable funding still remains several orbits out for most nonprofits. They focus only on making it to the end of the month or year. With this mindset of desperation and hand-to-mouth existence, picking the fruit—well before it is ripened—feels necessary.

But as soon as you shift to a mindset of contribution and abundance, a completely different way of approaching fundraising opens up. Rather than desperately and prematurely rushing to the Ask, a slower, more natural cultivation process makes sense.

Donors don't need to be strong-armed, tricked, manipulated, or made to feel guilty. These are donors who naturally want to give. They aren't giving solely because you ask them to; they're giving because they want to.

Rather than an external force (you) pushing them towards something they don't want to do, they are being pulled or "called" to precisely that thing that most inspires them. Their gift is so important to them that they aren't looking for any recognition.

I like to say that for these donors, it's as if they just sprinkled fairy dust on the most wonderful, deserving organization in the world. Their giving becomes a personal indulgence—a source of great pleasure and satisfaction.

This fundraising model was developed on a foundation of deep respect for donors and nonprofits alike. It teaches nonprofits to show people the value of their important work and naturally attracts individuals who are passionate about their particular cause.

Over the past ten years, the groups we have trained and coached have raised hundreds of millions of dollars, thanks to the training and rigorous coaching included in our Curriculum for Sustainable Funding. Our coaches hold people's feet to the fire to clarify and quantify their legacy of sustainable funding and then fulfill on it, financially.

In the process, seemingly amazing "side benefits" occur. Board members become more passionate, more dedicated volunteers show up, arts groups have more patrons and loyal subscribers, and the general community begins to understand the complex work of multi-faceted nonprofits doing advocacy and community development work, research, international relief work, etc. People tell us again and again that the model begins to affect—or perhaps, infect—everything, as it should.

For many groups that have been unable to participate in our programs firsthand, applying the model alone without the guidance of our expert instructors and coaches has led to a focus on the Ask Event. Often a lonely, hard-working, dedicated "self-implementer" is operating in a culture where the natural incentives are for a quick-fix, fast-buck solution. In that environment, it is no surprise that the Ask Event would become the primary focus.

Bringing about true change in the culture of an organization does not happen overnight. After nearly forty years in this field, I am enough of a realist to know that. Yet I do know that, fundamentally, people want what this model offers—long-term sustainable funding for the work of their precious organizations.

People want to see AIDS and cancer cured. They want to see people fed, educated, and able to support themselves and their families independently. They want to see global warming halted, a deeper appreciation for the arts, or a greater understanding among cultures and nations. They want to know that they are leaving this world a little better for their great, great grandchildren.

This book is an attempt to keep the larger conversation on course—to steer things back to the core conversation for sustainable funding, to remind people that there is life beyond the Ask Event. To let people step back and stop picking the fruit for long enough to cultivate the field and plant the seeds for future harvests; to leave a lasting legacy.

CHAPTER 1

THE HONEYMOON IS OVER

We hear it every day on our coaching calls with groups after their first successful Ask Event.

- *We did it! We had an amazing Ask Event.*
- *Our CEO said it was his best day in his twenty years with the organization.*
- *It put our organization on the map—it really told our story to the community.*
- *People were so impressed and inspired by what they saw and learned.*
- *Our board members couldn't believe it—they are so proud.*
- *We just did what our coach told us and it worked like a charm, just like you said it would.*
- *Our results even exceeded the formulas you gave us.*
- *We can't wait to do it again next year.*
- *All the hard work paid off.*

This is the standard refrain of our second-year groups. They did well. In many cases, their Ask Event was their single most profitable fundraising event ever.

Of the people who attended the Ask Event, 45%–50% made a gift that day, and 60%–80% of those donors were brand-new donors. Approximately 10%–15% of the guests joined the Multiple-Year Giving Society, making a five-year pledge to give $1,000 per year or more. It all seemed fairly easy and predictable.

This success makes many groups nervous. While it may look to the community as if the organization just raised a huge sum of money and must be "handled" financially, for many groups, the money raised in first-year pledge payments is still not enough to cover their "treadmill number" each year—that dollar goal they chase after to balance the budget.

Although they may have raised $100,000 at their Ask Event, that number includes pledges over the next five years. Their real first-year cash received may be only one-fifth of that, or $20,000. In other words, the model has not completely bailed them out for the year, and they need to do more fundraising, often of the old ilk—strong-arming and entertaining.

Now that these groups have seen the power of the model to produce mission-based donors and deliver on predictable formulas, they see where a little more work (for example, four or five more Point of Entry Events) would have yielded more money and more Multiple-Year Donors. They can see which steps of the model they skipped over or abbreviated in their rush to pick the fruit. They regret not having worked harder to secure a Leadership or Challenge Gift to announce at their Ask Event.

They know deep down that, in many cases, they were harvesting years of cumulative over-ripened fruit. They fear, and rightly so, that to keep the model growing, they are going to have to work harder to sustain these results next year and beyond. They worry about the payoff rate on their pledges. They wonder who is going to do all the follow up after the big event, as well as the cultivation necessary to grow these donors into major donors.

This is when we start hearing all the questions:

- *Now what? What do we do with these new donors?*
- *Do we send them an invoice each year for the next five years and then invite them back to our Ask Event in year six?*
- *Which portion of the event made it so successful?*
- *How do we do better next time with our Point of Entry Events?*
- *What were you saying about those Free Feel-Good Cultivation Events?*
- *What do you mean by cultivation, anyway?*
- *Now that we finally are able to justify hiring a new development staff person, what should that person focus on?*

- And most of all: *How do we keep the model going and growing towards our definition of sustainable funding?*

If they had a team working to put on the first Ask Event, some of the team members may want to move on to other pursuits. There may have been staff and leadership turnover. The model may have brought in new people with fresh energy, ready to become involved in significant ways. Where to begin to engage them in the midst of team turnover?

And, if the team is thinking about long-term sustainable funding at all, it is still no more than a dream, a fantasy that looms far away.

Life after the first year of implementing the model is still very much about survival.

Once the "high" of the Ask Event subsides, reality sets in quickly, and it's not always a pretty sight. The job of Team Leader or development director becomes very lonely. The honeymoon is over.

Right there on the phone, merely a few hours after their Ask Event, the coach walks the team through our detailed follow-up strategy and reminds them of the "no vacation after the Ask Event" rule. "This is the most fertile time for cultivation," the coach says. "This is when the donors are just getting excited about you. They have just discovered or rediscovered your work. They need to hear from you right away."

And for all those Ask Event guests who took their pledge cards home with them saying they needed to discuss their gift with their spouse, their board, or their accountant—who is going to follow up with them, and when? Everyone can feel the unrealized potential of the event that still remains. It is a time for getting to work, not resting.

The second round of money comes in through the mail. Checks from individuals, foundations, and corporate donors come in, along with all the wonderful (and sometimes critical) feedback from the board, staff, and volunteers. Tracking and accounting systems are often stretched to the limit.

It is in this post-Ask Event state of elation and exhaustion that groups walk into our 201 Workshops. They don't know what to do next. They are hungry for the next level of the model. They know what it's going to focus on: cultivation, one-on-one asking, and strengthening their Point of Entry Events. They finally see the importance of doing all the steps of the model, although they are overwhelmed by what that may look like.

Many of these groups don't fully understand the amount of work they still have ahead of them. They are at a dangerous place: thinking they understand enough of the model to be able to repeat their Ask Event success, yet knowing deep down that they could easily slip back to the short-term scarcity mentality.

We tell them that the second year—the 201 level—builds the bridge from the basics of the model to major gifts and beyond. And if you've ever looked at the underside of a bridge, it's not always pretty. It's complicated and hard work to build a bridge. You're fortifying and under-girding a major structure that will carry you forward. But in the end it will be worth it, because you will have built your pathway to major gifts, capital campaigns, and endowments. You will have a system for continually filling the pipeline with mission-focused donors. You will have a system for cultivating each donor through the process. And you will have a system for growing and refreshing your team to keep it all thriving.

The next level of implementation is truly not for the faint of heart; it is for the bridge builders, the people who are so committed and care so deeply about their organization that they are willing to work to ensure its long-term financial sustainability.

CHAPTER 2

REFOCUSING ON SUSTAINABILITY

Let's step back and put this all in context. Here are some questions to ask yourself:

What is so important about the work of your organization that you are giving your time to it?
Why are you doing all of this, anyway? What is it about your organization that captivates you? What is it about the work or mission that reaches deep into your personal values or background? Why would a person like you be involved with your organization? Why is it so important to you?

You have your own answer to each of these questions. Something in your family background or your life experience has brought you to or kept you at your organization. What is that?

It is important to acknowledge this driving personal motivator that keeps you involved and has you wanting the very best for your group. Namely, to be certain they can sustain themselves financially into the future.

We have the privilege of working with many founders, long-time CEOs, board members, and volunteers of nonprofit organizations—people who have dedicated their lives to a particular endeavor, like ending child abuse or finding a cure for a deadly disease that has affected them personally.

These are the people who wake up in the middle of the night worrying about how to fund the fulfillment of their mission. They know that they won't be at the helm forever, and they want to leave their successors the legacy of sustainable funding.

At one of our workshops, we asked everyone to consider their own personal motivation for being involved with their organizations, and Tom, a board member of an organization that provides community group homes for adults with developmental disabilities, told his story. Though Tom did not have any family members with developmental disabilities, his childhood best friend had a sister with developmental disabilities. Tom's friend had confided in him many times over the years about how concerned his parents were about who would look after her when her parents no longer could.

Because of that experience, Tom resolved way back then that if he could ever make a difference for people with developmental disabilities, he would. He doesn't want other families to have to worry about safe independent housing in the community for their loved ones. That is what motivates Tom to be involved with his nonprofit.

What's *your* story? What keeps you connected to your particular organization?

That personal commitment to finding the cure, ending child abuse, cleaning up the environment, or bringing the magic of the arts to the whole community is what will focus you and pull you forward along the path to sustainable funding.

Be forewarned: building sustainable funding requires a deep and enduring passion. Without that driving passion, you are better off sticking to the annual golf tournament or gala to help your group raise a good sum of money one year at a time and leaving the sustainable funding job to someone else. If this is merely a passing fancy or your project of the week, do not attempt this model.

If you have that passion and can tap into it, you are ready to move on towards sustainability.

What is the legacy you are committed to leaving your organization? What might happen if you made sustainable funding your legacy?
No matter how committed you are to this group, you aren't going to be around forever. What will be different there by the time you leave the organization? What would have to happen at your organization before you could turn over your role there and walk away with your

head held high? Perhaps it's a financial legacy—a certain amount of money to be used for a particular program or building. Or is it a particular program you want to see launched or expanded? Is it a huge endowment? Or a deeper reserve fund for emergencies?

What if you made sustainable funding your legacy? What if, rather than being dependent on the year-to-year, hand-to-mouth, survival-based approach to fundraising that has been used as the default since you arrived, *you* were the one to call for a new approach? What if that new approach allowed you to take your organization's financial future into your own hands, laying the foundation for long-term financial viability?

Take the time to imagine life at your organization without the worry that your largest funder might reduce your annual grant or cut you off altogether. Imagine being able to diversify your funding mix to significantly increase individual support. What if you could grow a reserve fund to tide you over when the next hurricane hits? What about building an endowment fund large enough to generate interest or investment income that covers the "treadmill number" that your organization struggles to raise each year?

These are the questions to ask yourself as you consider leaving the legacy of sustainable funding. If you care about your organization so much, wouldn't you want to leave it on a solid financial footing if you could?

How would you define sustainable funding for your organization?

Looking out over the next ten years, how would you quantify your definition of sustainable funding? How much unrestricted funding would you need each year? If you are looking to build an endowment or a reserve fund, how large must it be to generate enough investment income to significantly reduce (or even eliminate!) your anxiety about meeting your annual fundraising goal? Think big enough to get your organization off the treadmill.

This doesn't mean your organization will ever stop doing fundraising altogether. On the contrary, the very process of building towards sustainable funding will open up your group to the community in new and exciting ways. Your program goals will expand accordingly and the next level of fundraising may be needed. Yet the days of scarcity-based fundraising will be over.

For example, we work with a fifteen-year-old literacy program that needs to raise $100,000 each year in unrestricted funding. While they have done well at bringing in $20,000–$40,000 a year from one or two significant foundations and corporate grants, they still worry about becoming too dependent on these sources in the future. And the organization still has a big gap of $60,000–$80,000 a year to make up from special events, mailings, etc.

If they were to have an endowment fund of $2 million invested wisely, that endowment would generate $100,000 a year to cover their annual shortfall.

While $2 million is not a small amount of money for the literacy program to raise, the organization has many long-term supporters who have helped to keep the program afloat throughout the years. They believe enough in its good work; they see the long-term picture. If someone were to come to them with a well-thought-out plan for growing a $2 million endowment over the next ten years, they might very well want to contribute to it.

Someone has to be the whistle-blower on the one-year-at-a-time approach to fundraising. Like a loving parent who wants to see your children grow up and build a nice savings account to fund their retirement, you want your favorite nonprofit to be able to manage itself financially once you're gone as well. How would you quantify that?

What are your goals?
For groups that are serious about defining sustainable funding, we've created a chart that maps out the benchmarks.

OUR LEGACY OF SUSTAINABLE FUNDING

I. Ten-year goals

A. Total unrestricted funds we will raise each year over the next ten years.

1	2	3	4	5	6	7	8	9	10

B. In year ten, we will have a total endowment fund of $_____.
This fund will generate approximately $_____ per year in interest or investment income.

C. Sometime over the next ten years, we intend to have a capital campaign.
❏ Yes ❏ No   If yes, the amount we will need to raise for this capital campaign will be $_____.

Part I of the chart is all about your ten-year goals. Looking at the top row of numbers (I.A.), how much in unrestricted funding will you need each year? The literacy program predicted a 10% increase in their unrestricted funding needs each year. The first year, as we said, their need was $100,000 and by year ten, it had increased to $237,000.

EXAMPLE: LITERACY PROGRAM

A. Total unrestricted funds we will raise each year over the next ten years.

1	2	3	4	5	6	7	8	9	10
$100K	$110K	$121K	$133K	$146K	$161K	$177K	$195K	$215K	$237K

Now fill in the boxes in I.A. for your organization.

Moving on to the next question (I.B.), let's say your group decides they want to build an endowment large enough to generate your unrestricted funding needs for year one. That would be $100,000 each year in earnings you can live off of. Any additional unrestricted funding you need in subsequent years will come from continuing to use the basics of the model to bring in new Multiple-Year Donors, through Point of Entry Events, follow up, Ask Events, etc. In fact, some of these new Multiple-Year Donors could become endowment donors in the future. So your starting goal, assuming a 5% interest rate, is to have a $2 million endowment.

Here is a chart to help you calculate the size of endowment needed to generate your annual "treadmill number" of unrestricted funding.

GETTING OFF THE TREADMILL

Treadmill Number	Size of Endowment (at 5%)
$50K	$1M
$100K	$2M
$150K	$3M
$200K	$4M
$250K	$5M
$300K	$6M
$350K	$7M
$400K	$8M
$450K	$9M
$500K	$10M
$550K	$11M
$600K	$12M
$650K	$13M
$700K	$14M
$750K	$15M

Now you are ready to answer question I.B.: In year ten, we will have a total endowment fund of $_____. This fund will generate approximately $_____ per year in interest or investment income.

Next let's look at question I.C. What about a capital campaign? Is that in your organization's ten-year future? That new building or construction project to house your expanded programs may seem more attainable, now that you are beginning to see the "pipeline-filling" power of the model. How much would you need to raise through your capital campaign? Fill in your answer to that question.

Now, moving to Part II of the chart, let's look just at your next twelve months.

OUR LEGACY OF SUSTAINABLE FUNDING

II. Goals for the next year

A. Raise a total of $_____ from our Ask Event and related cultivation and Ask activities, including $_____ from Leadership/Challenge/major gifts.

B. Add _____ (number of) new Multiple-Year Donors to our Multiple-Year Giving Society. ($1,000 a year for five years = lowest level.)

C. Other goals:
   1. _____
   2. _____
   3. _____

Question II.A. introduces a new variable: the Leadership Gift, Challenge Gift, or major gift. This question asks: How much do you plan to raise from your next Ask Event and from the related cultivation and Ask activities, including $_____ from Leadership, Challenge, or major gifts?

Let's take that one step at a time. First, on the day of the Ask Event, how much do you plan to raise from the guests who are making new gifts and pledges that day? Let's say you're expecting $120,000. Next, what about the cultivation and asking you'll be doing of people who may not be able to attend the event, or people who come to the event but do not give that day? What about the people who take their pledge cards home with them and send in a generous gift after the event but before the end of your fiscal year? Those would be gifts coming from cultivation and Ask activities *related* to your use of the model. Let's say those non-day-of-Ask-Event gifts total another $50,000. So far, then, you are targeting to raise $170,000 at your next Ask Event.

Now, what about those Leadership or Challenge Gifts you will have secured prior to your Ask Event that will be announced at the event? A Leadership Gift is a major gift (ideally for the amount of your highest Multiple-Year Giving Society level or larger) from one or more individuals or foundations that is earmarked to be announced at your Ask Event in order to inspire additional giving. If it is an outright unrestricted gift from one donor, we call it a Leadership Gift. If it is an outright unrestricted gift from a group of donors, we call it a pooled Leadership Gift. If the gift is conditional upon being matched in any way at your Ask Event—by new multiple-year gifts made that day, for example—it is considered a Challenge Gift. In either case, it is large enough to be considered a major gift, and the people making the gift know that you will announce the total amount of the gift at the event, respecting their individual wishes about whether or not you name them as donors. (We will discuss Leadership Gifts and Challenge Gifts more in Chapter 9.)

Let's say, for the purposes of our example, that your board chair is very excited about the event and offers to ask the entire board to make a pooled Leadership Gift, with each board member contributing whatever amount they would like, and the total amount of the pooled gift comes to $30,000. This gift brings the total you are targeting to raise at your next Ask Event to $200,000.

Putting all of that together, your answer to II.A. would read:

Raise a total of $200,000 from our Ask Event and related cultivation and Ask activities, including $30,000 from Leadership/Challenge/major gifts.

Next is II.B.: How many new members of your Multiple-Year Giving Society do you plan to add next year? These are donors who pledge to give at one of your top three giving levels, the lowest level being $1,000 a year for each of the next five years. A good ratio is to predict that 10%–15% of the guests at your next Ask Event will give at one of these levels, assuming you have been doing the Point of Entry and follow-up work to properly educate and cultivate people before the Ask Event.

Finally, in II.C.: What else—besides money—do you want to accomplish in the next year by using the model? For example, do you want to open or expand a particular program, attract a certain number of new volunteers or supporters of your cause, add three new passionate board members, or engage a consultant to do a feasibility study for your future capital campaign? Make these items specific and measurable, not vague and general.

Although you may not see it yet, groups in our longer-term Sustainable Funding Program realize that by about year three of using the model, it has begun to impact and very naturally meld together everything they are already doing. So, thinking big with these "other" goals is a good idea.

Now that you know what you're aiming for ten years down the road, let's back up and see where you're really starting from.

CHAPTER 3

SUSTAINABLE FUNDING—
FROM DREAM TO REALITY

Lofty and idealistic as sustainable funding may seem for your organization, we say that achieving it is 90% science and 10% art. It can be predicted, measured, and tracked. If you are serious about full implementation of the model—well beyond the Ask Event—to achieve sustainable funding, the place to start is to rate your success against our Sustainable Funding Scorecard.

These thirty-three true or false questions highlight the specific mileposts on the pathway to sustainable funding. Our groups tell us this scorecard tends to de-mystify the process and provide a rigorous dose of reality as they measure and track their success with the model. While the list may seem a bit overwhelming, it can be divided into bite-sized chunks and prioritized.

SUSTAINABLE FUNDING SCORECARD

Mark each answer as "T" for True or "F" for False for your organization.
At the end, count one point for each "True" answer to get your score.

OVERALL
____ 1. A targeted measurable definition of sustainable funding you are aiming for

POINT OF ENTRY EVENTS
____ 2. **Sizzling monthly Point of Entry Events with at least ten guests per month in attendance**
____ 3. *25% of Point of Entry guests are referring others

*= key to leveraging the model; **bolded items = top 10**

---

continued on next page

continued from previous page

SUSTAINABLE FUNDING SCORECARD

FOLLOW UP

____ 4. Follow-Up Calls are made within one week of each Point of Entry; notes and next steps are tracked

MONEY RAISED FROM INDIVIDUALS

____ 5. Annual Ask Event that meets or exceeds the Benevon formula (e.g., 200 guests, $100K including pledges)

____ 6. **After year one, at least 40% of Ask Event attendees have attended a Point of Entry Event prior to the Ask Event ("ripened fruit")**

____ 7. 100% of Table Captains attended a Point of Entry prior to the Ask Event

____ 8. Less than 10% of Table Captains are staff

____ 9. Table Captain attrition at each year's Ask Event is 15% or less

____ 10. Percentage of no-show guests at Ask Event is 15% or less

____ 11. **At least 40% of Ask Event guests make a gift or pledge on the day of the event**

____ 12. 60%–70% of each year's Ask Event donors are new donors

____ 13. **At least 5%–10% of Ask Event attendees give at the $1,000 (for five years) level**

____ 14. ***At least 10%–15% of Ask Event attendees join the Multiple-Year Giving Society each year (at one of your three giving levels)**

____ 15. 30% of Table Captains join the Multiple-Year Giving Society each year

____ 16. 90% of pledges are paid off on time or early

____ 17. 10% of Multiple-Year Donors pay off their pledges in the second year

____ 18. 20% of Multiple-Year Donors increase or extend their gift each year

____ 19. 50% of year-one Multiple-Year Donors become year-two Table Captains

____ 20. 100% of year-one Multiple-Year Donors are invited to year-two Ask Event

____ 21. 80% of Multiple-Year Donors attend Ask Event in subsequent years as Table Captains or VIPs

____ 22. ***Challenge or Leadership Gift of increasing size at each Ask Event**

____ 23. Minimum of 10% increase in total budget dollars raised from individuals each year

____ 24. 100% board giving and at least 25% of board join Multiple-Year Giving Society

* = key to leveraging the model; ***bolded items = top 10***

continued on next page

continued from previous page

SUSTAINABLE FUNDING SCORECARD

CULTIVATION

____ 25. **At least two in-person or phone cultivation contacts with each Multiple-Year Donor each year**

____ 26. Annual Master Cultivation Calendar in place and being followed (even for donors who don't attend Free Feel-Good Cultivation Events)

____ 27. Two or more Free Feel-Good Cultivation Events per year with 50% of your Multiple-Year Donors attending at least one Free Feel-Good Cultivation Event each year

____ 28. **A sustainable tracking system used by everyone in the process to track all donor contacts**

TEAM

____ 29. A strong leadership team trained and coached in the next level of implementation each year

____ 30. Full support of the executive director and at least one board champion each year

____ 31. Increased board member passion and participation in the larger plan for sustainable funding

____ 32. **All new staff and board leadership trained in the model as they come on board**

____ 33. A leadership succession plan to ensure the team will continue to implement the plan for sustainability even as leadership changes

TOTAL

____ (maximum score = 33; or maximum score = 10 for the bolded items)

** = key to leveraging the model; **bolded items = top 10***

THREE KEY VARIABLES

There are three critical variables starred on the list that must be in place if you are to be successful in achieving sustainable funding. If you focus on these three variables, many of the other items on the list will "magically" happen as well.

The first of these three critical variables is **#3: 25% of your Point of Entry guests are referring others.**

Groups that regularly attain this standard find that everything else about the model glides into place. If your group is not having at least 25% of the people who attend your Point of Entry Events refer others to a subsequent Point of Entry, the problem is that your Point of Entry is not sizzling enough. While it may be enjoyable to you and a few of your inside staff, board, and volunteers, it obviously isn't getting the job done with the "real" guests.

Do not despair. This is a common problem. At our upper-level workshops, we often dissect Point of Entry Events under a microscope. We continue to find most Point of Entry Events over-inform and under-whelm their guests.

If a Point of Entry guest gets on a cell phone and calls a friend while leaving the event, saying, "You've got to see what I just saw," it is because they were sufficiently moved and excited by your work. People won't risk referring their friends to something that is just mediocre—it's got to be outstanding! Putting the sizzle into your Point of Entry Events is the subject of Chapter 6, but for now, let's just assume that your Point of Entry needs work to get it to the 25% referral level.

The second critical variable is **#14: At least 10%—15% of Ask Event attendees join the Multiple-Year Giving Society each year (at one of your three established giving levels).** If you can predictably count on meeting this standard each year, you do not have to ramp up the size of your Ask Event as a way to grow your numbers.

Knowing you will be adding new Multiple-Year Donors (who make five-year pledges of $1,000 a year or more) allows your giving society to grow over time and lets you focus more and more on these special major donors who have identified themselves as loyal supporters.

Rather than spending time making your Ask Event larger each year, you can focus on the other leverage points of the model—such as cultivating these prior Multiple-Year Donors to make subsequent Leadership/Challenge/major gifts, which can be announced at your Ask Event.

This 10%–15% standard is mandatory if you are planning to use the model to build sustainable funding.

The third critical variable is **#22: Challenge or Leadership Gift of increasing size at each Ask Event,** starting with a gift at least the size of your highest giving level. Like the other two critical variables, attaining this measure leverages the impact of the model in several ways. First, it gives you great confidence, walking into your Ask Event knowing that you already have at least one gift for $10,000 or $25,000 (depending on your highest giving level). Second, it inspires your Ask Event guests who may be impressed that you were able to get a gift of that size. Third, it honors the donor(s) and tells people that you have solid individual supporters standing behind you. That will give great confidence to other Ask Event guests who are considering a large gift, and for many donors who may never have regarded your organization as the place they would make their bigger gifts, it tells them that you have a larger plan—that yours is an organization worthy of larger gifts.

If this gift or pool of gifts is structured as a Challenge Gift to be announced at the Ask Event, it will leverage more large gifts on the day of the event. Many of our alumni groups have had the Challenge Gift donor(s) stand up at the event just before the Pitch to announce the gift themselves, saying that they made the gift in the hope that it would inspire people to give more today.

These reasons are all good, but the real purpose of this standard on our scorecard is that it pulls your organization forward into the world of major gifts. Without this requirement for an ever-increasing major gift, it would be easy for each group to regard their Ask Event as the trendy event of the year and miss its leveraging power to grow the model.

Having this requirement forces groups to begin to cultivate their Multiple-Year Donors quickly after their first Ask Event and to discern which Multiple-Year Donors have the capacity and passion to give more, well before their five-year pledge has been paid off.

By the time groups come to our Benevon 201 Workshop, having completed one successful Ask Event, they are often overwhelmed with what to focus on next. Requiring a major gift by the time of their next Ask Event pulls them forward quickly and helps them develop their list of Next Ten Asks, which will be discussed further in Chapter 9.

Just to reiterate before we move on to discuss the next tier of items on the scorecard: attaining these three critical measures over the next year is the single best predictor of your organization's likelihood of success in fulfilling your goals for sustainable funding.

THE NEXT SEVEN

The three critical variables, along with the "next seven" items, make up the top ten measures to focus on. These ten items are in bold type on the scorecard. The "next seven" are:

#2: Sizzling monthly Point of Entry Events with at least ten guests per month in attendance.

Ten guests per month is the absolute minimum. After the first Ask Event, most groups admit they did not have a Point of Entry Event each month leading up to the Ask Event. They know that they rushed to the Ask Event or picked the previously ripened fruit, without having done the necessary Point of Entry work.

By the second year, the model is far less forgiving. Without diligent focus on Point of Entry Events, your financial results will fall off significantly each year. Conversely, with a redoubled commitment to having those monthly Point of Entry Events, you will generate even more potential Point of Entry guests—more people excited about the organization and willing to invite others to attend these introductory events.

Even groups that diligently put on monthly Point of Entry Events usually see how they could put on more frequent events (two or three per month) and have more people attend each event. Many groups begin to see how to convert existing events (like volunteer recruitment events or community meetings) into Point of Entry Events, greatly reducing the work of finding people to come to these events each month.

#6: After year one, 40% of Ask Event attendees have attended a Point of Entry Event prior to the Ask Event. (20% is the minimum for year one; 40% for all subsequent years.)

We call this the "ripened fruit" formula, and it ramps up after year one from 20% to 40%. There is no substitute for a Point of Entry

prior to an Ask Event. You can work backwards from the number of guests you plan to have at the Ask Event to figure out how many people should attend your Point of Entry Events.

If you plan to have 200 Ask Event guests, you know that eighty of those people must attend a prior Point of Entry Event. Because only 25% of Point of Entry guests will actually end up attending an Ask Event, you can plan in advance to have 320 or more people at your Point of Entry Events during the year before the Ask Event.

While this may seem like a lot of work to attain the requisite eighty Ask Event guests, do not feel that you have wasted your time on those other 240 Point of Entry attendees. Some may never come to an Ask Event, but if your Point of Entry is sizzling enough, they may give one-on-one, and they will certainly refer others.

If your passion for the mission comes through at the Point of Entry, even the guests who choose not to become involved themselves will remember the impact of your work and mention it to others who might share a passion for your mission.

Furthermore, many Point of Entry attendees will want to become involved in other ways, perhaps volunteering in one of your programs, introducing you to their company or friend's work group or family, or helping with your fundraising efforts by hosting a Point of Entry for their friends or family.

Of course, the eighty people in this example who do attend the Ask Event after coming to a stellar Point of Entry and receiving personal cultivation will be some of your biggest donors at the Ask Event and beyond. Many will be Table Captains at your first event and for years to come. It all starts with that sizzling Point of Entry.

#11: At least 40% of Ask Event guests make a gift or pledge on the day of the event.

This should not be hard to attain if you have been meeting the other measures on the scorecard. In fact, we are always suspicious of groups that exceed 40% by too much. We will discuss this more in Chapter 12 where we cover tips for your subsequent Ask Events.

I like to see 40%–50% of the guests giving on the day of the Ask Event. That tells me that no one felt pressured to give. If the percentage is higher, the gifts are often for smaller amounts and the total raised at the Ask Event can be much lower. This 40% rule ties in closely to the next measure.

#13: At least 5%–10% of Ask Event attendees give at the $1,000 (for five years) level.

Adding new members to your Multiple-Year Giving Society at this entry level of $1,000 a year will provide a steady stream of new donors to be cultivated towards even larger gifts over time. Although you might think that meeting measure #14—having 10%–15% of your Ask Event attendees join your giving society each year at one of the three established levels—would be sufficient, we have found over the years that some groups actually have an easier time picking the "ripened fruit" at the higher donor levels ($10,000 or $25,000 a year for five years). While we certainly want you to keep cultivating and asking for those larger major gifts, we also want to make sure you keep your eye on the ball of these most precious "new baby" major donors at the $1,000 a year level. That way your pipeline will be filled as you build towards long-term sustainability.

#25: At least two in-person or phone cultivation contacts with each Multiple-Year Donor each year.

As mentioned earlier, many groups ask us if they should just invoice their Multiple-Year Donors for the next five years and then invite them back to their Ask Event in year six!

On the contrary, regular personal cultivation of the Multiple-Year Donors begins right away, with the Five-Step Follow-Up Call within a week of the Ask Event.

Two in-person or phone contacts a year is the bare minimum. Notice that newsletters, printed invitations, and mailings do not qualify as cultivation contacts in our definition. We will discuss how to customize each cultivation contact in Chapter 8.

#28: A sustainable tracking system used by everyone in the process to track all donor contacts.
Sustainable funding requires a sustainable tracking system that will live on long after you're gone. It needs to track every contact with each donor. To be consistent with our model, there are several other requirements of a tracking system. We will cover these in Chapter 18.

#32: All new staff and board leadership trained in the model as they come on board.
You need everyone to understand how the model works and what their role is in its successful implementation. No one should be forced to participate—they just need to understand the basics.

Ideally, they will see how this fundraising method treats donors the way they like to be treated. There are many easy ways for new people to learn the basics of the model—online or through our other publications.

MOVING FORWARD AS A TEAM

Now that you have learned the ten key variables on the Sustainable Funding Scorecard, go over these measures with the rest of your team. This scorecard is an excellent starting point for a team discussion. Take the time to mark each item true or false, and you will have identified the areas you need to improve as you move forward with the model.

CHAPTER 4

REVISITING THE MODEL

After the first Ask Event, people begin to realize the extent to which the model begins to affect everything: volunteer recruitment, community support, media recognition, and staff morale.

People also see where they may have hurried over aspects of the model in order to get to the Ask Event.

Now that you have answered the questions on the Sustainable Funding Scorecard, you no doubt see some places where you could deepen your implementation of the model. Let's walk through the model together one more time, just to highlight some of the sand traps that have snared even our most dedicated groups.

This will also be valuable for those of you who may have joined an implementation team without ever having a formal orientation to the model.

Recall that the Benevon Model is a four-step circular process—like an old-fashioned toy train track—for building long-term relationships with mission-centered individual donors: people who truly believe in the work of your organization.

By following this model over time, it begins to spiral up. Many of these mission-focused donors will choose to stay with you forever.

Eventually, the model becomes the operating system—like an operating system on your computer—that can hold all your other programs, such as direct mail, special events, major gifts, capital, and endowment.

STEP ONE: THE POINT OF ENTRY

Potential donors get on the track at a Point of Entry. This one-hour introductory event educates and inspires people about your organization. You do not ask for money at a Point of Entry. You should assume that potential donors will attend only one Point of Entry Event in their lifetime, so it should be memorable.

A Point of Entry must include three components:
1. The basic "Facts 101" about your organization, including the vision and the needs.
2. An "Emotional Hook" so compelling people will never forget it.
3. A system for "Capturing the Names" and contact information of the guests, with their permission.

As individuals, we are emotional donors looking for rational reasons to justify our emotional decision to give. In other words, your Point of Entry must satisfy both the head and the heart; neither the emotion nor the facts alone will do it.

STEP TWO: FOLLOW UP AND INVOLVE

The second step is Follow Up and Involve, which begins with a personal Follow-Up Call within a week to each person who attended the Point of Entry Event. This is not just a standard thank you, for which a note would suffice. It is an interactive research call. It generates an authentic dialog with true give-and-take.

The Follow-Up Call follows a specific, five-point format:
1. **"Thank you for coming."**
2. **"What did you think?"** Ask enough questions to get them talking.
3. **Listen.** The more you listen, the more you will notice that potential donors are telling you exactly how they would like to become involved with your organization.
4. **"Is there any way you could see yourself becoming involved with our organization?"**

5. **"Is there anyone else you think we should invite to a _____ (Point of Entry Event)?"** People will have been so inspired by what they learned that, even if they choose not to become involved themselves, they will likely know someone else who would.

Do not assume that everyone who comes to your Point of Entry will want to become more involved with you. For those people who tell you they are not interested, you will "bless and release" them. Thank them sincerely for taking their time to come and, graciously, let them go.

The Cultivation Superhighway

In the old reality, the Ask often happened too soon, before the person had a chance to buy in, head and heart, to the mission of the organization. In the new reality, asking is more like picking the ripened fruit from a tree. By the time you get around to asking people for money, it should be nothing more than "nudging the inevitable."

On the other hand, if you wait too long, the fruit becomes over-ripe, falls to the ground, and spoils. In the life cycle of each donor, there are perfect moments for asking for money. You have to tune your radar to those moments.

In this model, everything between the Follow-Up Call and the Ask is called the Cultivation Superhighway. The more contacts you have with potential donors along the superhighway, the more money they will give you when you ask. There is a direct correlation between the number of contacts and the size of the gifts received.

The best types of contacts are personal and focus precisely on what the donor told you they were most interested in during the Follow-Up Call. If, for example, a donor said he or she would like to help you expand a program, you would need to invite the individual back to meet with the key staff in that area, with the board, or with the director—the more meaningful the contacts, the better. Contacts are what ripen the fruit.

STEP THREE: ASKING FOR MONEY

When you are sure the donor is ready to be asked, there are two ways to accomplish this: one-on-one in person and/or at the Free One-Hour Ask Event. The Ask Event connects both new and former donors to the powerful work of the organization and its impact on the lives of real people. The well-choreographed program sequences the larger vision with facts, emotion, testimonials, and video. The critical mass of true believers in the same room will produce remarkable results in just an hour.

Whether one-on-one in person or at an Ask Event, each Ask must include two essential ingredients:

1. Inviting people to become part of a Multiple-Year Giving Society by making a multiple-year pledge to support the unrestricted operating needs of the organization. This allows donors to declare themselves as part of your organization's family. It gives a particular group of more committed donors the opportunity to say, "You can count on me. I'm a long-term believer in what you are up to." It allows donors to "go public" with their commitment and support by naturally sharing their enthusiasm for your program with others.

2. Asking for specific levels of contribution, which we call Units of Service. These are the bite-sized chunks of unrestricted funding that one person can support. They relate to the needs that were clearly identified at the Point of Entry and at every contact along the way. There should be only three Units of Service, and the lowest level should be $1,000 a year for five years.

STEP FOUR: INTRODUCING OTHERS; RECONNECTING EXISTING DONORS

In the fourth step of the model, individual members of the Multiple-Year Giving Society introduce others to the organization by inviting them to Point of Entry Events. Since your donors have been through the cycle with you, they know you will take good care of their friends, and they hope those friends will fall in love with the organization and become lifelong donors themselves.

To keep your donors in the cycle, every Multiple-Year Giving Society Donor is invited to two or three program-related Free Feel-Good Cultivation Events during the year, such as graduation ceremonies or special celebration days. Donors are encouraged to invite others to these Free Feel-Good Cultivation Events (also called Point of Re-Entry Events).

Following the Free Feel-Good Cultivation Event, every donor receives another one-on-one Follow-Up Call asking a few more open-ended questions and giving them the opportunity to suggest others who might like to be invited to a Point of Entry Event.

The cumulative effect is clear, as this simple circle becomes a spiral with an ever-growing number of Multiple-Year Donors who give increasing amounts to support operating needs, capital, and endowment. These will be donors who have chosen to contribute for the right reasons and who will stay with your organization for a lifetime.

Now, let's move on to deepening each step of the model, starting with the Point of Entry.

CHAPTER 5

TELLING THE TRUTH
ABOUT YOUR POINT OF ENTRY

The number one "mea culpa" we hear from groups after the first Ask Event is, "We wish we had held more Point of Entry Events. Now we see why they are so important. We were in such a hurry to get to the Ask Event, and we knew we had plenty of people who already knew about our good work, so we never really focused on our Point of Entry."

In other words, if their Ask Event met our formulas for dollar results without having had the requisite number of prior Point of Entry Events, they got lucky. Generally, these groups recognize that they had plenty of pre-existing ripened fruit to get them through their first Ask Event, but for the second time around and beyond, they are going to have to do the real Point of Entry work.

While this is a scary thought for these groups, this "a-ha!" about lack of Point of Entry rigor is critical after the first Ask Event. If they don't get to work now to improve their Point of Entry, their results each year will diminish greatly. It motivates groups to get serious about designing and testing a succinct one-hour Point of Entry that is so good that guests feel compelled as they leave to get on their cell phones and call people saying, "You've got to see what I just saw. This place is amazing."

If your Point of Entry was that good, you'd have a natural engine—a feeder system—for bringing in new people to your organization, month after month, year after year. And when you have an airtight system for putting on stellar Point of Entry Events at least once a month, you will be able to make this model self-sustaining within your organization.

Said another way, if you don't have a brilliant Point of Entry that continually generates new people coming to subsequent Point of Entry Events, you are not truly following the model. The Point of Entry is the very heart of the model and is—by far—the most important step. It is the gas pedal that drives the model. It is the pipeline-filler for future donors. It keeps this circular model going round.

As we often tell our groups in our workshops: "If you are going to adopt this model to build long-term sustainable funding, you are going to be putting on Point of Entry Events for the rest of your organization's life! So stop the worrying, and let's get to work designing a Point of Entry that works every time."

EVALUATING EFFECTIVENESS

To evaluate the effectiveness of your organization's Point of Entry, start by checking your answers to the two questions on the Sustainable Funding Scorecard in the Point of Entry section:

- Do you have sizzling monthly Point of Entry Events with at least ten guests per month in attendance?
- Are 25% of your Point of Entry guests referring others?

Your answers to these two questions directly correlate with one another. Let's look at why.

The number one reason we hear from groups to explain why they are not having monthly Point of Entry Events with at least ten guests in attendance is that they can't find enough guests. And the most common excuse for why attendance is poor is because "our board just isn't inviting people." It is no surprise, then, to hear that these are the same groups that aren't getting the 25% referral rate after their Point of Entry Events.

Conversely, groups that meet one of these measures usually meet the other one easily. For some groups, having at least ten guests per month happens very naturally, and they readily achieve the 25% referral rate as well. Their boards are happy and not feeling pressured to invite anyone to anything. Why is that?

Rather than focus on pointing fingers, blaming, and feeling guilty, look to the real problem: the content of your Point of Entry. Digest this fact, plain and simple: *If you're not getting 25% of the people who come to your Point of Entry Events happily referring others to attend, it means that your Point of Entry is not sizzling; it is just "nice."* A nice Point of Entry is not what someone wants to refer their friends to. It's got to be life-changing and truly memorable—something that makes the guests feel compelled to get on their cell phones immediately after the Point of Entry to tell their friends and family about it.

You also need to digest the fact that you are not the best person to rate just how much your Point of Entry sizzles. You are too close to your organization's daily work and larger mission to be able to rate your Point of Entry objectively.

Think about how little it takes to get you excited about the mission of your organization. You already know so many of the issues related to it. You have a wealth of stories, memories, statistics, and case examples all built up around this cause you are so passionate about. When a brand-new person walks into your Point of Entry, you are like a little kid wanting to jump up and down and say, "See! Isn't this great work we are doing? Let me tell you about it."

In other words, it is impossible for you to be objective and put yourself in their shoes—you already know too much.

Let's step back and address these issues one at a time.

Our Point of Entry Isn't Sizzling; It's Just Nice

First, what do we mean by sizzling? We mean memorable, compelling, and gripping. It's got to leave a visceral imprint on the guest—something they will never forget. The event even needs to move those of you who organize and speak at the Point of Entry, no matter how many times you have experienced the event before.

The event needs to tug at the heartstrings several times by including four or five stories. Each story needs to include at least one fact that conveys the needs and the gap between where you are now and your dreams for the future. The facts must make it clear to your guests that, while you have a plan and vision for the future, you are not going to get there on your own. You need their help to fulfill the plan.

In addition to inspiring people, the Point of Entry needs to let each guest know that you would love to have them get more involved with your organization, in whatever way works for them, including referring others who may have an interest in your type of work.

Guests need to know that no matter how nice your surroundings look, you are not "handled." The mission you are here to fulfill still urgently needs them: you haven't cured the disease yet, ended child abuse, etc. There's still more work to be done.

I recall an exceptional Point of Entry I visited for a residential treatment home for children who had been abused and neglected. It had a wonderful theme—hands. I was greeted at the front door by an adult and child. The child took my hand and walked me over to the sign-in table. I was both physically and emotionally "touched" from the minute I arrived.

There were handprints of children used as metaphors throughout the Point of Entry. As victims of abuse, these children had come to associate hands with bad things. This residential program aimed to transform that image for these children. They wove this theme into the stories told, and we viewed pictures of handprints in the bedrooms and hallways as we toured the building.

The most memorable moment for me was the finale of that Point of Entry. Each guest was escorted by a child to a tray filled with colorful finger paint, where we got to make our own handprint on a big group poster. I will never forget that little five-year-old boy holding my hand proudly as we walked over to the paint, rolling up my sleeve, covering my hand with the slippery red paint, pushing down on the back of my hand to be sure every single digit was imprinted on the paper, and then walking me over to the bucket of warm water, washing off the paint, and carefully drying my hand.

Before I left, I knelt down and gave him a hug, thanking him for the wonderful experience. It was such a proud moment for this child to know he had made a difference with me. Talk about memorable! It had been a long time since I'd done any finger painting, and the love and care that little boy took in helping me make a beautiful handprint spoke volumes about the work this organization does every day.

Unfortunately, not all the Point of Entry Events we visit are that sizzling. Although our groups often give themselves high marks when they rate themselves on their events, our coaches don't always agree. We see Point of Entry Events that may be technically correct in that they follow the proper one-hour agenda, but they don't knock your socks off.

These lackluster events leave guests saying, "What an interesting group. Those people obviously know what they're doing." But guests aren't compelled to take action. Guests need to leave your Point of Entry saying, "I have to tell people about this," or "Wait until I tell Jane—this is just the kind of thing she would love."

In other words, even if guests choose not to become personally involved, they should be so excited about what they saw that other people will come to mind who they would like to tell about it: people for whom your issue is "just their thing."

One line that is a good indicator of having a memorable, sizzling Point of Entry is when people leave saying, "I had no idea you did all this here!" That tells you that they truly learned something new, expanded their thinking, and grew in their understanding of your work or issue in the world.

People Aren't Referring Others

The second problem people commonly have with their Point of Entry Events—referral rates—is directly related to the first. Without a stellar, sizzling Point of Entry, your guests will be reluctant to refer others. When you call your Point of Entry guests to follow up within a week after the event and ask them that final question on the Follow-Up Call script, "Is there anyone else you can think of who we should invite to a Point of Entry?" they reply, "Let me think about it," or "I'll get back to you." But they never call you back.

Groups that are not meeting the 25% referral rate also find they need to rely heavily on their board members to invite people to Point of Entry Events to make up the gap. If, after the first year of implementing the model, you are still looking to your board to do the majority of inviting of people to Point of Entry Events, you should probably take that as a sign that your Point of Entry is lackluster.

Put yourself in the place of your guests. Would you refer a friend to something that was just "nice"? You would want your friend to be happy with you—to come back saying, "Thank you for encouraging me to go visit that amazing organization. It's exactly the kind of thing I had been looking to get involved with. I never would have known about it if it weren't for you."

It's not that your guests don't have friends who care about the type of work your group does. It's that they don't want to jeopardize referring a friend to something that's not really great. If your Point of Entry is truly powerful, people will be happy to hear from you in the Follow-Up Calls. Right away they will say, "I'm so glad you called, I've been thinking about that event ever since I came to visit. I have some people I'd like to invite to see what I saw. How would I go about doing that?" In some cases, they will be calling you before you call them!

The good news is that a sizzling Point of Entry Event is possible for every single nonprofit organization, regardless of the mission, type of work, size, location (or lack of one), etc. Once you understand what we are aiming for in a Point of Entry, you will see ways to improve yours. That will get the spiral going in the right direction, with Point of Entry guests happily referring others.

Let's move on to dissecting your current Point of Entry and adding that sizzle, and then we'll discuss how to design a system for having a steady stream of Point of Entry guests.

CHAPTER 6

DISSECTING YOUR POINT OF ENTRY—ADDING THE SIZZLE

In this chapter, we will dissect and reconstruct your Point of Entry agenda. This chapter is for groups that already have a Point of Entry they want to improve, not for groups that need to design a Point of Entry from scratch.

(Note: If you are looking for a detailed manual for how to design a sizzling Point of Entry from start to finish, read *The Point of Entry Handbook*. There you will find many sample Point of Entry formats for different types of nonprofit organizations. Each type of organization has its own challenges, be it location, multiple programs, or time of day. Those challenges are addressed in detail in *The Point of Entry Handbook* and will not be addressed here.)

As we walk through the Point of Entry agenda using the chart on the next page, rate the various elements of your existing Point of Entry as if you were a brand-new guest.

POINT OF ENTRY IMPROVEMENT PLAN

	Current Rating (1-5)	Modifications to be Made	Next Actions	By When?
Venue				
Time of Day				
Greeting, Sign In, Mix & Mingle				
Welcome				
Visionary Leader Talk				
Top Three Programs, Myth-Buster Facts, Handouts				
Emotional Hook (Essential Story, Live Testimonial)				
Thank You, Wrap Up				

VENUE

Let's start with the venue—where to hold your Point of Entry Events.

If you are still struggling with a venue for your Point of Entry Events, you should figure out a way to have them be great right in your own office, even if your office seems small, messy, or boring to you.

The classic Point of Entry Event is a tour. Even if you think there would not be much for people to see on a tour because your work is confidential or takes place offsite, you can create a virtual tour right in your office or conference room, using photos, stories, and live testimonials or letters from staff or clients. That way you can test and refine each element before you take it on the road to board members' conference rooms, church basements, or corporate lunchrooms.

Even if you decide later to do the majority of your Point of Entry Events in an offsite location, I recommend you continue to offer as many Point of Entry Events as you possibly can at your offices or main location.

TIME OF DAY

This takes some experimenting, so please don't lock into a time of day until you have tried a few options. Consider convenience for your guests and the best time of day for people to be coming to see your offices, especially if guests will be able to see your programs in action. What kind of programs would you like them to see? When do the mentoring sessions happen? What time of day is best to tour that particular program? When will the staff be there to visit on the tour and tell a story? Would a weekday or evening work best? How about a weekend day?

GREETING

Imagine that I am your brand-new Point of Entry guest. Who greets me as I arrive? Is it a friendly person who I will see again during the hour? Is that person wearing a name badge to help me remember her name? Does the greeter tell me how she's involved in the organization to ensure the personal connection?

SIGN IN

Is the sign-in process pleasant? Am I told that I am being asked to provide my information so you can get my feedback on the whole experience? Am I informed that your organization is trying to learn how best to communicate your work in the community?

MIX AND MINGLE

During the mix and mingle time, as we are waiting for the other guests to arrive, what am I looking at? Is someone pointing out things to me like the new paint or new programs or a project that is just beginning? Am I told how it got funded and how grateful your group is for that funding? And am I, perhaps, told that it is just one of several similar projects you would love to complete in the future to allow you to serve more people?

In other words, make sure that you are helping me connect the dots right from the start. While I am standing in a conference room or lobby waiting for the Point of Entry to begin, you know that I am in one of your group's three locations in the county. Are you telling me that? Are you saying what goes on in this building? If clients are arriving, is someone pointing out to me what they are coming here to do?

I will be noticing the quality of the interaction with your staff and how warm and receptive your staff members are. And later, when you tell me that you have a shortage of speech therapists for the children because you aren't able to pay the going salary, I will understand the human impact.

WELCOME

Ideally, the opening welcome is done by a board member. In the (rare) absence of a board member, another volunteer welcomes people. Do not have a staff person do the official welcome.

Here is the script for your welcome person to follow:

Thank you all for coming, and thanks to the person who invited you here today. We are delighted you could join us! We have put this hour together so you and others in our community have an opportunity to learn more about our work here at _____. We hope that you will become more knowledgeable and inspired about our work, as inspired as we all are every day. We will look forward to your feedback.

Then the greeter should tell their own personal story about why they work or volunteer with your organization, before they introduce the Visionary Leader.

Questions to ask in rating your welcome: Does the welcome person seem to really care about this organization? Does she tell me a story that explains why she cares?

What is her personal connection to your organization? Perhaps her child or parent has been a recipient of this program. I want to know about the real impact your organization is having in the world.

VISIONARY LEADER TALK

After the welcome, the first speaker at your Point of Entry is the Visionary Leader. To review, the Visionary Leader is the top-ranking staff member, usually the executive director or CEO. If your organization has no paid staff, then the Visionary Leader is the top-ranking volunteer, usually the board chair.

On the next page is the outline for the Visionary Leader Talk—the questions in each section are designed to help you fill in the blanks and prepare a great talk.

The real power of the Visionary Leader Talk is in making it personal. It's got to come from the heart. Regardless of the style or personality of your Visionary Leader, this person's passion for the work needs to come through, starting with the Visionary Leader's own personal connection.

At our 201 Workshops, we have a very special breakfast meeting just for the Visionary Leaders where they tell us their personal stories. Their commitment is palpable, and they are hungry for coaching to do whatever it will take to make them more effective in telling their stories. These are high-level CEOs who are not accustomed to showing emotion in a professional setting. Yet at this breakfast, once they see and hear what we are aiming for in another person's talk, they quickly see how to tell their story authentically in their own voice and how to coach others in strengthening their delivery.

VISIONARY LEADER TALK OUTLINE

I. Personal story (1 min)
   A. What personal incident or experience brought you to this organization in the first place?
   B. What keeps you working there?

II. Mission/history of the organization (1 min)
   A. When was it founded? By whom?
   B. Why does the organization really exist?
   C. What values does it teach, encourage, or represent?
   D. How has it evolved and grown since the beginning?

III. The gap (2 min)
   A. How many people are unserved or underserved now?
   B. What is the impact on each guest of the absence of those needed programs and services in our community?

IV. Vision for the future (2 min)
   A. What will it take for you to fulfill your mission?
   B. Where do you want to be five to ten years from now?
   C. If you accomplish your goals, what will be the impact on the broader community?

Notice that the entire talk lasts no more than six minutes. Only one minute of the six is to give the standard background facts and figures about the organization. And even then, there are many ways to spice those facts up with human stories or examples that bring them to life.

A full two minutes is dedicated to talking about the gap between where you are now and where your organization would like to be. As a Point of Entry guest from this community who doesn't know you very well yet, I should start to see how closing that gap will make my life better, even if the problem or issue doesn't affect me directly.

And, finally, share your vision for the future. Tell me the day-to-day things you struggle with. Those are the things that will cause me and others to jump in and help. Tell me specifically what it will take for you to fulfill your mission. Where do you want to be five to ten years from now?

Paint a clear picture and a pathway, but let me know that you will need some help to get there. If you leave me thinking you've got it all handled, I will move along to the next organization. Let down your hair a little and tell me your struggles—be human.

In rating your Visionary Leader Talk, here are some things to consider: Is this person genuine and believable? Does this person's passion for the cause come through? Can I tell that that spark of passion drives this person every day? Do I understand why this issue or cause is so important to this Visionary Leader?

Regardless of their speaking ability, can I tell that this person knows what they are doing? Is this someone who will be a good steward of my money if I choose to give here? Does this person have a clear and solid vision for fulfilling the mission of the organization? Or is this person just treading water, doing their best with an intractable problem?

The Visionary Leader Talk should cause me to ask myself what specific needs your organization has that I could fulfill—tangible goods like used computers or books, skills I could bring like advice on improving your accounting systems, or contacts with other people I could easily lead you to. It should inspire me to look at your Wish List.

I should be compelled to wonder how I can make a real difference with this group. I should feel that this Visionary Leader is someone I would want to introduce to my friends and colleagues. The Point of Entry should call me to action.

HANDOUTS

Fact Sheet

Next on the program, the development director talks for a maximum of five minutes about your programs and the facts about your work. The bullet points on the accompanying Fact Sheet handout highlight your top three programs and memorable facts and statistics that open people's eyes to your work. It is easiest if the development director just walks people through the Fact Sheet, item by item.

The Fact Sheet lists the answers to two or three of your most frequently asked questions. Questions like:

- Where does the money come from?
- How do people get referred to you?
- How much is the tuition to go to this school?

The Fact Sheet should contain the questions you get asked so often, you get tired of answering them because they seem so basic.

Here is a worksheet to help you identify your top three programs and myth-buster facts that will be included on your Fact Sheet. Whether your organization is small and single-focused or large and multi-faceted, it will take some work to zero in on the simplest way for people to get to know you.

TOP THREE PROGRAMS AND MYTH-BUSTER FACTS

TOP THREE PROGRAMS
When listed together, these programs must convey the breadth of your work.
1. _____
2. _____
3. _____

TOP THREE MYTH-BUSTER FACTS
What are the three biggest myths or misconceptions about the people you serve? What fact would dispel each myth? Be sure each fact helps to convey the gap or need. These will answer some of the questions you are frequently asked.

1. Myth: _____
   Fact: _____
2. Myth: _____
   Fact: _____
3. Myth: _____
   Fact: _____

If you have many programs and don't know where to begin, look to your mission statement. Odds are this will be the overarching reason for housing so many programs within one organization. You should be able to state your mission and programs succinctly. Beware of jargon and acronyms that people won't understand—terms like "victim mediation" or "DRGs."

Make sure that the three programs convey the breadth of your work and the ongoing needs of the people you serve. For example, a group serving adults with disabilities has jobs, housing, and arts programs. See how succinctly that can be said?

When it comes to myth-buster facts, what are some of the facts and statistics that would surprise people and dispel some of the myths about your organization or the population you serve?

For example, a widely-held myth about Habitat for Humanity is that they give away houses for free to needy people. In fact, they build houses in partnership with the working families who pay to live in them, both with their own sweat equity and with low-interest loans.

To further convey the need, Habitat for Humanity tells people that they need building materials donated and that they need volunteers to work alongside the families to keep housing costs low.

They tell Point of Entry guests about the number of families on the waiting list and the difference it would make in the lives of those families to have a safe and secure roof over their head every night—a home of their own to get them back on their feet.

Do not overdo the use of graphics on the Fact Sheet. One pie chart or bar graph is sufficient—just be sure it teaches me something and opens my eyes further to your needs. For example, a chart showing the percent of your budget that has been affected by government funding cutbacks or the number of students in your job training programs who are employed within six months versus the results of other similar programs.

Now, stand back and assess your Fact Sheet and the way you present your top three programs and myth-buster facts. Do they give me a good range of the organization's services? Could I walk away and tell a friend about your organization's scope of work and the impact of one or two of your specific programs? Do they teach me new information and convey the organization's deeper needs to me? For example, I may be thinking that this regional food bank looks like a sophisticated major wholesale distribution center that has plenty of money, great systems, and all of their needs met. What more could they possibly need from me?

When I hear that over 40% of their clients are working families of three people or more earning an average of $11,400 a year, that dispels the myth or stereotype some people may have of a chronic, "lazy" welfare recipient who just likes to take from the government.

When I hear that the average age of a food bank recipient is ten years old and that, for many of these fourth graders, their school lunch is their only meal of the day, I think of the impact of hunger on children.

When I hear the gap between the number of people in need of food every day right in my city or state versus the number served by this regional food bank, I see the need.

Other Handouts

Although you will not be going over these in detail during the Point of Entry, the development director or person who covers the top three programs and facts needs to call people's attention to the other one or two handouts they received. These are the Wish List and, optionally, your basic brochure.

Wish List

Your Wish List is the handout that people will zero in on. Many of your Point of Entry guests will want to help you right from the start!

Make sure your Wish List contains items you really want, because there's a good chance you'll be getting them. Include ten items at the most. It's fine to put in volunteer positions like a volunteer coordinator or people to help you host and organize future Point of Entry Events.

Many groups are concerned that they don't have ready-made volunteer roles for the people who will want to become involved after a Point of Entry. Do some creative brainstorming with your staff to see what other real needs they can identify.

Be sure not to put any dollar amounts on anything on your Wish List. This is not the place to ask for money or to identify how much your needs will cost.

Basic Brochure

The brochure is a nice touch, but optional. If you have such a brochure, this is the time to use it. It doesn't need to be the fancy, four-color version—just your basic version will do. Many groups don't have a brochure, in which case, the Fact Sheet and Wish List will suffice. Do not go to great lengths to have the perfect brochure for your Point of Entry.

Now, rate this element of your Point of Entry program, from the perspective of your guests.

EMOTIONAL HOOK

Strengthening Your Emotional Hook

While the warm welcome and facts will impress people, the one thing that will make your Point of Entry truly sizzle will be the stories that convey the human impact of your work.

Remember that as individuals, we are emotional donors looking for rational reasons to justify our emotional decision to give. Some groups worry that if they incorporate too much emotion, it will seem contrived—their guests will feel that they are being manipulated or that your clients are being exploited. In fact, your guests want to know how your work affects real people. Unlike those of you who work day to day at the organization, your Point of Entry guests do not wake up every day thinking about the emotional impact of your work. They need you to help them make that connection at each Point of Entry Event. You need to spell it out with examples and stories.

I will caution again that you are likely not the best judge of the depth of emotion present at your Point of Entry. Most of our groups truly believe that their Point of Entry is already emotional enough. But by our standards, they are barely scratching the surface. *We have only one test for sufficient emotion: are you getting the 25% referral rate after each Point of Entry?*

Can you list at least three times where your Point of Entry connects people to the emotional impact of your work?

While, for most groups, the Emotional Hook is conveyed during the tour or virtual tour, through stories and testimonials, if you want your Point of Entry Events to really sizzle, you should infuse emotion into every aspect of the one-hour event, from the minute a person walks through the door, until you say goodbye to them at the end of the hour.

To get into the right frame of mind for this, think about what keeps you involved with this organization. The reason for your involvement will probably involve a story—either your own or someone else's—that you will never forget. What is that personal connection that causes you to stay there, day after day? What little successes show you that you are on the right track to solving a bigger problem? Those are the stories you will want to convey to your Point of Entry guests. And to the extent that you hold back on delivering the full emotional impact of your work, your Point of Entry will just be "nice" as opposed to stellar.

People need to leave with their eyes open wide to the issue you're addressing, stunned by the challenges you face every day, and grateful that your organization is doing this work. That's what will compel them to take action. Beware of the temptation to over-inform and under-whelm people. Facts alone are not enough. You've got to move people.

Part of moving people might be making them a little uncomfortable with how the issue your organization addresses affects them personally. It's not enough for them to feel badly for the people you serve. That still keeps the issue at arm's length from them.

You've got to help people make the connection between the kids served in your inner-city teen mentoring program and the lives of their own kids out in the suburbs. It is not enough to have them see that your work is good for society in general. How does it affect the child sitting next to their child in school or the mother of their employee who might be calling in sick if your program weren't there to support her?

If I were a guest at your Point of Entry tour, what might I notice as I'm walking around? I see the pictures and thank-you notes from grateful families tacked to the walls in the staff cubicles, stacks of court files filled with paperwork about how to get each child out of foster care and into a permanent home, and a teddy bear on the floor.

All of my senses are engaged as we tour the dining room at the senior day center where each senior is partnered with a high school student who is talking with them and helping them with their lunch. I see people laughing and talking. This is much different from what I had expected to see.

At the theater, we stop on the tour to have the artistic director tell us about his first memory of visiting the theater as a young boy growing up on a farm outside of town. He explains how it changed his life forever. And then we meet the stage crew and one of the actors who stops to tell us how he got involved in this work. Holding their scripts and props, we have a new appreciation for their passion and for the amount of work it takes to put on the amazing productions this theater is known for.

With the Christian school's choir rehearsing in the background, we hear a testimonial from a grandmother who talks about how she can rest easy each day at her job, knowing that her grandson is being loved and educated at this wonderful inner-city Christian school in a way that is consistent with her values.

Because the organization with small-loan programs has offices all over the world, we hear letters of gratitude from women in impoverished countries and see pictures of them standing beside their new homes, thanks to this small-loan program in their village.

We hear the sounds of the rainforest in the background on the audiotape as we sit in a California living room, awed by the stories and facts about what is happening to the rainforest and the people whose lives are integral to it.

In every case, guests are hearing stories—Essential Stories—about the lives being changed thanks to the everyday work of this organization and its dedicated people.

The Emotional Hook needs to ooze into every aspect of the Point of Entry. Each person's passion needs to come through.

Refining Your Essential Story

Do you have an Essential Story? If not, you need to find one. If you have one already, now is the time to refine it. Although it is just one of many stories you will tell in many ways at your Point of Entry Events, having an Essential Story helps you prepare other stories. It gives you a template for how to tell powerful stories throughout the process.

The Essential Story follows a particular format. Learning that format and writing your primary Essential Story will help you to tell many other stories using this same approach. Once you have taken the time to write out one story succinctly, you will see how tricky it can be to get it right.

Recall that the Essential Story has three stages: the Before, the Intervention, and the After.

THREE STAGES OF AN ESSENTIAL STORY

ELEMENTS	SAMPLE PHRASING
Stage 1: Before	
• Choose one person's story. • Briefly describe their situation before working with your organization. • What was their life like then? How difficult was it?	I'll never forget the story about Tom. Just a few years ago, Tom had a family and a job. Through a set of hard circumstances, he found himself hopeless and living under a bridge. He had fallen about as low as you can in our society. When I tell this story, it always reminds me of how much I take for granted in my own life, like a roof over my head, a hot shower every day, or even a hot meal. It is hard to imagine how he survived day-to-day.

continued on next page

continued from previous page

THREE STAGES OF AN ESSENTIAL STORY

ELEMENTS	SAMPLE PHRASING
Stage 2: Intervention	
• What brought this person into contact with your organization? • What services and support did they receive from you? • What was your personal observation of them at that time?	Someone mentioned to Tom that he could get a decent meal at our shelter. I will never forget the look in his eyes the first time he visited us. He was so embarrassed to have to take what he called a "handout." Every day Tom came to the shelter, he gained strength. He started to talk to others at the dinner table. We helped him learn computer skills so he was able to get a job in a new field. We provided hope for him. We helped him regain a sense of pride and self esteem. He was so proud of what he was accomplishing. I saw him in class one day tutoring one of the other new students who was struggling to learn to use the computer keyboard.
Stage 3: After	
• What are the results of the intervention? How has life changed for this person? • What is now possible for them? • What does this person now say about their life? • How are they "giving back"to others?	Getting involved with our organization gave Tom a new future for his life. Tom is thriving now. He has an apartment, a job, and seems to be on top of the world. He volunteers with us when he has the time. He walked up to me a month or so ago, gave me a big hug, and told me that our organization had literally saved his life. He drives by that bridge every now and then and it reminds him how lucky he is. He says he won't quit until everyone under that bridge gets the same chance he did. This is what people tell us all the time: "You people know no limits to caring."

Here is a basic, fill-in-the-blanks template for you to use in writing your Essential Story. Once you have finished it, read it out loud and time yourself. It should be no longer than two minutes. It needs to both showcase your work and move people who hear it to tears.

In other words, the story also teaches people what you do. So be sure to highlight that middle part of the story, what we call "the intervention," and find a way to detail the unique services your organization provided to turn those lives around.

Take the time to fill in the blanks in the template. It will get you started on having a terrific Essential Story.

ESSENTIAL STORY TEMPLATE

I'll never forget the story about _____

1. Before _____ (name) found (came to, got involved with) _____ (our organization), her life was _____. So many of the things that you and I take for granted, such as _____ _____, just weren't possible for _____ (name). It seemed to _____ that this would never change.

2. _____ found (came to, was referred to) _____ (our organization) by _____. Within _____ months (years), _____'s life turned around. Rather than _____ _____, she was _____. Our _____ (specific, jargon-free) programs taught _____ to _____ and helped her get back on her feet again. People who saw _____ back then said she was _____ (a changed person, full of life again, able to look you in the eye). Really, what we provided her was _____ _____ (a sense of pride, dignity, confidence, strength, courage) to get back out there and be a good _____ (parent, student).

3. Now, _____ is thriving. She has (is, does) _____. She says life will never be the same. Every time she thinks about (goes back to) _____, she says she thanks _____ for (giving her back her pride, her children, saving her life, her education, her dignity). The last time I saw her she was _____ (or: she came back to see us recently and said _____).

   _____ is just one example of the lives that are being changed every day here at _____.

Live Testimonial

Including an optional, live testimonial at the end of your Point of Entry adds a powerful, distinctive Emotional Hook that people will never forget. It can also be risky and add a layer of anxiety to producing an easy, repeatable Point of Entry. And if you have done a great job telling stories throughout your Point of Entry tour, ending with a live testimonial may seem like too much.

If you are considering including a live testimonial in your Point of Entry, I recommend you start by making a list of people who would be good Testimonial Speakers, people who have compelling stories to tell—both consumers of your services and your staff. Interview them in person and have them tell you their story. Coach them and have them write it down. Find out how often they are available to tell the story. You can ask them to come to certain Point of Entry Events and not to others. A client testimonial can also be written as a letter and read by a staff member at a Point of Entry with a very dramatic effect.

No Video

Do not use a video at your Point of Entry Events. Save your video for the Ask Event. It is far better to have your Point of Entry guests hear testimonials from real people. You want your Point of Entry guests to feel that they are getting a special, up-close look at what you do, and video or PowerPoint presentations tend to put guests at an arm's length distance. Think of your Point of Entry like a personal gathering around your kitchen table. You wouldn't stand up at the table and start a PowerPoint presentation or a video; it detracts from the natural, personal feel.

THANK YOU/WRAP UP

The wrap up is often done in the lobby as people are finishing the tour. You do not need to bring people back into the main room to regroup for the wrap up. Usually the board member or the person who did the initial welcome is the person who does the wrap up. Here is a script for what they say:

Thank you, once again, for joining us here today. We can see that some of you have been truly moved and inspired, as we are, by this work. We are looking forward to hearing any questions and comments you have as well as your feedback and advice about how we are sharing our message. We will give you a call in the next few days. Thank you all, and have a great day!

These comments will be most effective if they include a genuine and enthusiastic thank you. It is truly a gift to your organization that these guests are taking their valuable time to come and learn about something new, and it's worth recognizing that.

It is also helpful to let them know in advance that you hope they were inspired today. This is the place to warn them that you will want to get their advice to help you learn how to better tell your story in the community and to be thinking about anyone else they know that might enjoy coming to take the tour. In the closing remarks, you simply tell them you will be calling for their feedback. You want to hear their opinions.

Notice that none of this wording mentions fundraising. That is not meant to be a trick. It's because you really aren't looking for money at this stage of the process. You are just looking for people who are passionate about the specific mission of this organization.

From a guest's perspective, at the end of the hour, am I left with new questions unanswered? Am I surprised by how quickly the past hour has flown by? Did I learn new things and have my view of this issue greatly expanded? Am I thanked by that same volunteer or board member who welcomed me initially, but this time I feel more connected to this person? Do I want to know more?

And as I leave, I should be saying out loud: "I had *no idea* you folks did all of this here—this is really amazing, and thank you for opening my eyes to this. I would love to talk to you further; please give me a call."

If this is the case, the Point of Entry has done its job. It has educated and inspired me without asking me for money. I have willingly given you my permission to contact me again soon. It hasn't pressured me in any way to do anything more. It was a real eye opener, and it knocked my socks off.

As I leave, I am sorry that it's over. I pick up my cell phone to call someone close to me to share what I learned. "You've got to see what I just saw. This place is amazing!"

PULLING THE PIECES TOGETHER

Does your Point of Entry live up to this standard? Chances are that you still have areas that need work. Let's take a closer look at ways to improve the various elements of your Point of Entry to increase your impact and make your Point of Entry more memorable.

Before we move on to increasing attendance at your Point of Entry Events, go back to the Point of Entry Improvement Plan at the beginning of this chapter and add in your next steps for refining and upgrading each part of your Point of Entry. Fill in all the remaining columns on that form.

CHAPTER 7

ENSURING STEADY
POINT OF ENTRY ATTENDANCE

Now that you are excited about your sizzling Point of Entry, how are you going to ensure a steady stream of guests who are genuinely interested in learning more about your work? Furthermore, how can you put in place a system for generating Point of Entry guests without relying on board members to keep inviting their friends?

The first answer should be obvious. The Point of Entry Events will be so inspiring, so life-changing, that at least 25% of your guests will be referring others. You will follow up to ensure that those "others" actually attend subsequent Point of Entry Events, either escorted by their friend or alone. Once the model gets working smoothly, these "others" will get excited and at least 25% of them will, in turn, refer the next ripple of "others" and so on. Because you will "bless and release" people liberally along the way, thanking them for coming to your Point of Entry and for referring their friends, you will constantly be culling out the people who are less interested in your mission and continuing to cultivate those who *are* truly interested in moving forward with you.

As the model grows, year after year, with regular Point of Entry and Ask Events, new people will naturally be added to the mix. Your radar will become finely honed for people who have not yet been to a Point of Entry or who could refer others to attend. Your Point of Entry will get better and better with practice, and it will take on a life of its own. Rather than happening once a month, your events will become more frequent. Twice a month, once a week, and before you know it, you will find ways to turn your other events and public presentations into Point of Entry Events. Be it a volunteer recruitment meeting, a pre-gala party for your volunteers, or the lunch at the end of the golf tournament, you will see ways to include the Facts 101 and Emotional Hook elements of the Point of Entry in every event you're already doing.

Whether or not these other events qualify as bona-fide Point of Entry Events, they now include a mission-focused program element, connecting the guests to the real work of the organization. You'll begin to identify the many things your organization is already doing that can be re-infused with your mission, thus generating even more guests for your "real" Point of Entry Events.

This Point of Entry infusion does not have to be random and haphazard. Like everything else in our model, over time, the Point of Entry system will become as routine and natural as your procedures for delivering your other programs.

WORKING THE NUMBERS

Organizations that have adopted the model over many years find that they can plan the date of their Ask Event a full year out and then, working backwards, know the number of Point of Entry guests they must have in order to generate sufficient new Table Captains to keep their Ask Events fresh each year.

To truly systematize the process and integrate it into the fiber of your organization, it is crucial to calculate the numbers for filling your Point of Entry Events and ultimately your Ask Event—in other words, to blend your Point of Entry guest strategy with your Table Captain recruitment plan.

Once groups come to terms with the number of Point of Entry guests they need to generate sufficient Table Captains and Ask Event guests, they often start having Point of Entry Events more frequently—two to four times per month. Depending on how soon their next Ask Event will take place, they work backwards to calculate the number of Point of Entry guests they need to ensure that at least 40% of their Ask Event guests will have attended a prior Point of Entry. For example, if their next Ask Event is ten months away, and they want to have 200 people in attendance, at least eighty of them (40% of 200 guests) must have been to a Point of Entry.

We assume that, worst case, out of every hundred Point of Entry guests, only twenty-five will actually end up attending the next Ask Event. Half of them, or fifty, you will have "blessed and released" either because they never returned your Follow-Up Call or they told you they were not interested in becoming more involved (though they may have referred others).

Of the remaining fifty who are interested in becoming more involved, twenty-five won't make it to the Ask Event for one reason or another. They may RSVP yes and then need to cancel at the last minute due to illness. Or they may tell you right away that they will not be able to attend the Ask Event because they will be on vacation, have another commitment, or they are just not an event-going type of person.

Accept the reality of the 25% conversion ratio of Point of Entry guests to Ask Event attendees and plan accordingly. In our scenario, we are looking to have a 200-person second-year Ask Event. In order to ensure that eighty of those 200 people have been to a prior Point of Entry, ideally in the past twelve months, we will need to have 320 Point of Entry guests in the next ten months. That is an average of thirty-six guests per month.

While that number sounds large, imagine for a moment the impact of having thirty-six Point of Entry guests per month. The word about your organization would spread quickly. Again, whether or not those guests all choose to become involved, they will be spreading the word about what they learned at your Point of Entry. They will tell their colleagues at work. Perhaps they work at a company or live in a community that takes on a community project each year.

While some guests may not think they are getting involved with you directly, they will be referring you to larger networks and groups that you can subsequently invite to Point of Entry Events or take a Point of Entry on the road to their homes or workplaces. It won't take long before your organization becomes better-known in the community.

If you keep your Point of Entry Events going at this pace, you will no longer be the "best kept secret" in your community. The investment of time and energy you have put into ramping up the model in your organization will start to pay off.

With a goal of 320 Point of Entry guests in the next nine months, you would be wise to plan more than one Point of Entry per month. Since the ideal Point of Entry size is ten to fifteen guests, you will need three Point of Entry Events per month in order to accommodate thirty-six guests per month.

Three Point of Entry Events per month—how might that look in your organization?

One strategy might be to have two Point of Entry Events in your office and one on the road, perhaps to a brown bag lunch series for employees of a company where one of your advisory committee members works.

Another strategy might be to have two "standard" Point of Entry Events at your office and convert another standard monthly event, like your monthly volunteer recruitment meeting or member recruitment event, into a Point of Entry.

EXPANDING AND DEEPENING YOUR TREASURE MAP STRATEGY

After your first Ask Event, you should not need to rely on board members and staff to supply Point of Entry guests. That is not a sustainable strategy. To actually achieve the Point of Entry guest number needed to meet your next Ask Event goal, the place to start is by refreshing your Treasure Map annually to include a broader mix of groups. This will happen naturally if you just follow the process.

Go back to the Treasure Map you made when you first started having Point of Entry Events. (For complete instructions on how to make a Treasure Map, see the Appendix.) Even if you took the time to make a good one, odds are it has been collecting dust somewhere in a closet. As a starting place, take a good look at your original Treasure Map again with your team. Then put it aside, and start a new one.

Making a Treasure Map as a team provides the "a-ha!" moment for most groups. Beware: do not try to make a Treasure Map for your organization on your own. You can certainly practice this exercise alone or with family or friends, but in order for this to be a useful and effective resource, you ultimately need to do this exercise with a team of people with diverse roles within your organization. Include representatives from groups like your program staff, volunteers from different aspects of your services, administrative staff, and former and current board members.

If you are unable to get everyone together all at once to make this expanded Treasure Map, it is fine to meet with groups individually so each can make their own Treasure Map. Then these separate maps made by program staff, board members, volunteer tutors, etc., can all be consolidated into one composite Treasure Map for the entire organization.

What is a Treasure Map? It is a representation of the web or network of groups and individuals who already know and love your work plus others who would have a reason to say yes when invited to attend a Point of Entry. While that may sound like nearly everyone in the community, in fact there are some people or groups of people who would be more likely than others to care about your work. Those are the people to put on the Treasure Map—the ones who are more inclined to like your work. And there are plenty of them out there!

If you have already made a Treasure Map, here is a way to take it to the next level of complexity. As with a full Treasure Map, start by drawing a small circle and putting the name of your organization in the middle of that circle.

TREASURE MAP
GROUPS AND ORGANIZATIONS

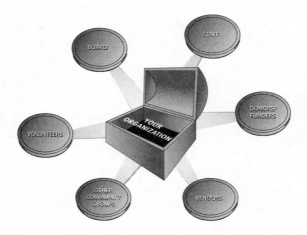

Next, add in the names of the groups or organizations you come in contact with on a regular basis, like volunteers, staff, board members, donors.

Now, make a satellite Treasure Map branching off from the first one. This satellite map will focus on one of those groups—for example: your donors.

This addition of a second tier to your Treasure Map allows you to get more specific and detailed in your analysis.

In this example, we added many types of donors on the satellite Treasure Map: Multiple-Year Donors, donors to your capital campaign, one-time donors, corporate donors, foundation donors, and direct mail donors. Around volunteers, you could draw a satellite Treasure Map of all your volunteer groups, like volunteer tutors, volunteers in your soup kitchen, fundraising volunteers, etc.

TREASURE MAP
DONORS AND VOLUNTEERS

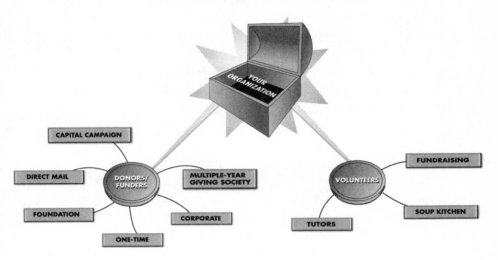

Each of those groups is filled with people who already know and love your organization—and who know other people they would be happy to invite to Point of Entry Events. The natural passion of the people in these groups will come through to their friends when they invite them to come to your events.

The friends they invite will be inclined to say yes, mostly out of guilt and obligation. In other words, while the mission of your organization, be it ending child abuse or savoring local history at your museum, may not be their particular passion, they will come to the Point of Entry because they won't want to say no to their friend who is so excited about your work.

Once they attend your sizzling Point of Entry, even if they are the people you "bless and release" because they choose not to become involved, they will have been sufficiently inspired by your work and will likely know of others they could refer to attend a future Point of Entry Event. Don't be surprised, however, by how many of these friends of your Treasure Map groups will, in fact, choose to become more involved of their own accord. After all, your organization has a valuable mission in the world, and there are plenty of generous people out there looking to become involved with your meaningful work. They just didn't realize it until they attended your wonderful Point of Entry!

If you do this second tier Treasure Map off of each primary group on your main Treasure Map, you will see that you have an abundance of people to invite to your Point of Entry Events.

CHOOSE FOUR TARGET GROUPS

Next, to help you focus, choose four target groups from your Treasure Map. Focus your efforts on these four groups in the coming year. For example, you could zero in on your former walk-a-thon participants, the alumni of your girls' program who are now corporate executives, your past board members, and your "special grandparent" volunteers.

If you set a goal of having a certain number of Point of Entry guests from each of the four categories and focus solely on those categories, you will have a plan. If your Point of Entry is stellar, these people will naturally want to refer their friends to attend as well.

When you meet the goals you have set for the number of Point of Entry attendees you plan to have from each group, you will have generated so many new referrals and passionate new supporters that you will be ready to make a whole new Treasure Map by the end of the year.

Rather than defaulting to pressuring your board members to invite their same friends and colleagues who will feel obligated to give you money, you will discover—very naturally—the many new groups of individuals who actually want to become involved in your organization's work.

The rich treasure that has been lurking outside the doors of your organization—mostly in the form of people's passion and participation—will have permeated the fiber of your organization. You will have new volunteers, new and recommitted board members, and an infusion of new energy into your existing dedicated team.

After making your new tiered Treasure Map, use the form below to bring some reality to this process by identifying the four target groups from your Treasure Map that you will be focusing on this year. Then, make a list of at least twenty people from each group that you could invite to your Point of Entry Events.

TABLE CAPTAIN STRATEGY

1. Today's date: _____
2. Month/date of Ask Event: _____
3. Targeted number of guests at Ask Event: _____
4. Number of Table Captains you must start with: _____
5. Minimum number of guests who must attend Point of Entry (at least 40% of #3 above): _____
6. How many Table Captains will come from each group on your Treasure Map? _____

Treasure Map Group	Names of Potential Point of Entry Guests				Targeted Number of Potential Table Captains
			Total Table Captains:		

In Chapter 13 about your Ask Event projections, we will discuss how to use this focused strategy to fill out the last column above: targeted number of potential Table Captains.

POINT OF ENTRY HOSTS

Another way to increase your Point of Entry guest numbers and the number of events you hold each month is by having people host whole Point of Entry Events. The obvious place to start is with your board members, but if this is your second year or more with the model, you should plan that only one or two board members will really come through with hosting and filling an entire Point of Entry for ten to fifteen people. Ask at a board meeting if anyone would like to do this. It will need to be a person who has attended a prior Point of Entry and loved it.

If you followed the model in year one, you put on a "kick-the-tires" Point of Entry for your board. It is now time to do that again. Once a year, have a Point of Entry just for your board. Those board members who attended the prior year's "kick-the-tires" event will be delighted with the refinements and improvements you have made (often in response to their feedback!) and once again be reconnected to their passion for your work. They may be inspired to invite others to your regularly-scheduled Point of Entry Events or even to host a Point of Entry of their own. Your new board members will be equally (or even more) excited and agree to do the same.

Some groups bring a calendar to one board meeting each year with the schedule of the next full year's Point of Entry dates and ask board members to sign up to host one event per year. This doesn't necessarily mean being responsible for filling the entire Point of Entry with ten to fifteen people. It is much less intimidating for them to attend as the host who welcomes guests at the start of the Point of Entry on behalf of the board. Of course, if the hosting board members have people they would like to invite, that's great too!

Another approach is to have the board collectively host one Point of Entry per year. Let's say it is in the month of June. You can either keep it at your normal time during the day or make it a special early evening event, adding light food and a thirty-minute optional social time before the actual Point of Entry begins. One of the board members who is a big champion for the Point of Entry Events should coordinate this effort, starting with setting a goal for the number of people you would like to have at the event and getting the June date on the calendars of all the board members.

As we have said, the board will quickly become burned out if you rely on them too heavily as your Point of Entry hosts and your source of Point of Entry guests. You will need to expand beyond the board to find Point of Entry hosts. This is where your Treasure Map comes in. Two of the best groups you should be able to add to your Treasure Map now that you have completed your first Ask Event are your prior year's Table Captains and your new Multiple-Year Donors.

You could ask each of your prior Table Captains and new Multiple-Year Donors if they would be interested in hosting a Point of Entry or pairing up with someone else to co-host a Point of Entry. After all, these are people who have expressed a serious commitment to you, with their time and money. They are true believers in your work. It would be natural for them to want to share it with others.

Regarding prior Table Captains at your Ask Event, you can expect that 25% of them will become repeat Table Captains at next year's Ask Event. For many busy people who love your organization but do not have time to get more involved day to day, serving as a Table Captain offers the perfect amount of focused effort and rewards them with a wonderful one-hour event where they are reconnected to what they love so much about your group.

Once you tell these loyal Table Captains that you want to have 40% of their guests each year attend a Point of Entry prior to the Ask Event, you can ask them if they would like to host a special Point of Entry just for their friends. Or if they are super-busy or just don't want the responsibility of organizing a private Point of Entry like this, your organization can host a larger Point of Entry just for prior Table Captains and their potential guests. That way, the Table Captains can reconnect with fellow Table Captains as well as introduce new people to your Point of Entry, without having to organize the entire Point of Entry themselves.

Another often overlooked group of potential Point of Entry hosts are your recent, excited prior Point of Entry guests. If your Point of Entry is knock-your-socks-off terrific, people will leave so excited that they will naturally want to tell others, beyond giving you a name or two of a friend or colleague. Often they will be part of a personal, professional, or community group that they could easily invite to an upcoming Point of Entry. Here's a tip: add to your Wish List at your Point of Entry that you are looking for people to host other Point of Entry Events. If you are rigorous with this, you may well be able to have at least one Point of Entry per month this way.

Another strategy for getting to the requisite number of Point of Entry guests per month is for your organization to host selected Point of Entry Events aimed at targeted Treasure Map groups such as retired people, young professionals, people in a particular faith community, etc. Identify a leadership volunteer or team of volunteers who will agree to invite that group to this special Point of Entry.

HOW TO INVITE POINT OF ENTRY GUESTS

Remind those people who agree to host events or to invite friends that the Point of Entry is not a fundraising event; their friends will not be asked for money at the Point of Entry. Give them the script for inviting people to a Point of Entry (see Appendix).

Your goal is to get the word out about your work. You want people's feedback and advice about the event afterwards. Tell Point of Entry hosts and inviters that each guest will receive one Follow-Up Call after the event. If the guest chooses not to become involved, you will "bless and release" that person. You will only cultivate and further involve those people who expressly tell you they would like to become more involved.

In other words, reassure the people (particularly board members) who are inviting guests that this Point of Entry is not a shortcut for strong-arming, manipulating, or tricking their friends. It truly is intended just to get the word out about your work.

Next, talk up the Point of Entry plans and progress at board meetings, particularly if this is leading up to a special Point of Entry being hosted by the entire board. Have board members who have invited guests to Point of Entry Events in the past speak about how much their friends enjoyed the experience and how it allowed them to connect to the mission of the organization in their own right. You can even circulate a list of the confirmed guests to date (along with the name of the board member who invited each of them) at every board meeting.

Board members who really love your organization, but are reticent to ask their friends for money outright, will love this type of event. It allows them to play the role we feel is most critical for your board members: the role of an ambassador for your group in the community. And that does not necessarily require that they ever ask anyone for money.

SYSTEMATIZING THE POINT OF ENTRY PROGRAM

Having an unending stream of people to invite to Point of Entry Events goes a long way towards ensuring the system will live on. There are a few more things to mention, related to the program itself.

Once you have refined the content and format of your Point of Entry so that it works every time, generating the 25% referral rate, with at least one full Point of Entry of ten to fifteen people per month (or enough to provide the requisite number of guests needed prior to your next Ask Event), you need to be sure the production of the Point of Entry is simple and repeatable with the least effort on everyone's part.

At the school where the model was started, our Point of Entry Events caught on so well that there were many weeks leading up to our first Ask Event when we held three or four Point of Entry Events. Thankfully, by then, we had our routine figured out. All of the handouts and paper supplies were kept in a box in a closet in the lunchroom where we held the Point of Entry Events. The kitchen staff brought out a pitcher of orange juice and a plate of fresh fruit and muffins thirty minutes before starting time.

The board member hosting that event arrived thirty minutes early also. Our Visionary Leader arrived five minutes before starting time, to greet people warmly, and stayed for the first twenty minutes of the event, to do the Visionary Leader Talk and answer a few questions. Our sign-in person was our volunteer coordinator, who was a volunteer herself. She came fifteen minutes early, set up the sign-in table (using the table and supplies in the box from the closet). She stayed through the entire Point of Entry so that at the end if people were interested in getting more involved by volunteering, they could talk with her right then.

Occasionally, at the end of the Point of Entry, people stuck around to talk. We had allocated the hour after the Point of Entry for the head of the school (the Visionary Leader) to be available to meet with people if they were really excited and wanted to talk to him right away. Usually we were able to screen those requests so it took a minimum of his time. Most days, the event was finished and cleaned up, with the box returned to the closet, by fifteen minutes after the event ended.

Given the scale of the implementation of the model at the school where this all got started, we had over 1,100 guests in the first five months of holding Point of Entry Events! Had I stopped to count them along the way, I probably would have keeled over from exhaustion.

But because of our smooth system for putting on the "show," it never felt like a burden. On the contrary, we were all so energized every morning. That energy infused each day, which was just what we needed to make all those Follow-Up Calls and to begin the cultivation process.

CHAPTER 8

THE SCIENCE OF "SPECIAL"

The only way your organization will ever be able to grow the model to its potential (and meet the rigorous measures on the Sustainable Funding Scorecard) is by mastering the cultivation process. Whether you are aiming to grow your Point of Entry guests into Ask Event guests and Multiple-Year Donors, grow your Multiple-Year Donors into challenge and leadership donors, or grow your challenge and leadership donors into major gifts, capital, and endowment donors, they will only proceed around the circle with you if you tend and nurture their unique interest in your work.

While it is easy to feel overwhelmed and burdened by the thought of having to cultivate so many people at so many different levels, it is worth stopping to recognize how far you have already come, by following a step-by-step process—a system.

Can you see that if you had a similar step-by-step process for cultivation, you could gradually ramp up the entire model to the next level and begin to experience the spiraling effect that our upper-level groups all talk about?

We refer to this process—this personalized cultivation system—as the "science of special," and just like the rest of the model, it is highly effective if you take it one step at a time and follow the system.

WHAT DO WE MEAN BY "CULTIVATION"?

For each donor, everything that happens between the Point of Entry Follow-Up Call and the Ask (either one-on-one or at the Ask Event) is what we call the Cultivation Superhighway. That careful listening during the Five-Step Follow-Up Calls, when each person tells you if and how they might see themselves becoming more involved with your group, determines the next step you will take with them.

It's as if a good friend of yours stopped by your office, you took some time to show him around, and the next time you talked to him, you thanked him for coming by and asked what he thought. Imagine that he immediately zeroed in on the environmental program, which is one of many programs you offer. Even though you would have other priorities for growing other programs first, you would never think of derailing your friend into another program area. You would invite him back to meet with your great staff members who are working on the environmental program. Over time, if gently nurtured with occasional phone calls, e-mails, and face-to-face contact with your program people, scientists, and students, your friend would become more and more engaged in your work. He would contribute naturally that which he has in abundance—his knowledge, passion, contacts, time, and, when asked to make a longer-term financial contribution, he would naturally sign on for five years and probably offer to be a Table Captain at your Ask Events each year.

Over the years, he would get to know many of your staff and volunteers. He would have helped to grow your environmental program. He would have involved many of his friends, inviting them to Point of Entry Events and letting you follow up to determine how they might like to become involved. His relationship would be with that aspect of your mission that most mattered to him. He would stay involved because your group's work is important to him, rather than out of any sense of guilt or obligation to you.

Likewise, you would have gotten to know him better. You would know his family situation and, eventually, his giving capacity. He would likely become a board member or honorary advisory committee member. When you launched your endowment campaign to ensure the future of the organization, you would be sure to talk with him and his family about a named family endowment structured to sustain the environmental program into the future.

That simple, natural, organic flow of contacts and communication is what we call cultivation. At Benevon, we define cultivation as tending, growing, and nurturing something gently over time. More specifically, cultivation in our model looks like many contacts with a donor in the course of a year—each one highly customized to that donor's particular interests, needs, and style. There is not a simple template for donor cultivation other than this simple mandate: it's got to be personal!

Think about a favorite cause that you give to. Perhaps you send in a small check each year or give online after a disaster or at holiday time. Maybe you give to your alumni association in response to a phone-a-thon or to your church's annual stewardship program. Regardless of the size of your gifts, your name is undoubtedly on one or many donor lists. If they are doing their jobs well, good people in nonprofit organizations are thinking right now about how to cultivate you in the very best way, over time, to have you consider making a larger gift to their group.

If you are giving because you have an emotional connection to their work, not just because someone pressured you to give, you may be starting to realize how little those organizations would need to do to cultivate you to give more.

I have often told the story of the search and rescue group that rescued my sister and her husband in a remote mountain area many years ago. Though all they do is send me a letter and an envelope each year, the letter always includes a story of another death-defying search and rescue effort that ended happily, and that one mailing a year is always enough to inspire me to give, often at a higher level than the year before.

Then we have the story of my husband, who is a long-time donor to our (now grown-up) son's little league baseball team. Though they would never know it other than by my husband's modest annual (and totally unsolicited) donation to them every year, that team is very near and dear to his heart. They accepted our son onto the team because there was no official team in our neighborhood. Well beyond teaching baseball, they taught him the values of true sportsmanship, leadership, and teamwork that have served him immeasurably as he has grown up.

In both cases, my husband and I give because we truly believe in the work of these two organizations. Yet with just a little cultivation from these organizations, we could become far more involved and give even more.

In contrast, there are also the groups that badger us, calling incessantly, sending us mailings too many times a year (or even right after we have made a large gift). Would we call these letters and calls "cultivation"? Not in our model.

Think about how you like to be treated as a donor, with all your quirky and not so quirky preferences. Like me and my husband, your preferences may change as your life situation changes, depending on the organization and other things you may be involved with at the time.

The point of all this: there is no such thing as one-size-fits-all cultivation. It has to be tailored and customized to fit each donor. This is one more reason to get to know your donors personally and to listen as closely as you can—to discern their particular preferences about how they want to be cultivated by your organization.

CONTACTS ON THE CULTIVATION SUPERHIGHWAY

The road markers along the Cultivation Superhighway are contacts. Each contact your donors have with your organization gently nurtures them along the path. We say that there is a direct correlation between the number of cultivation contacts you have with a potential donor and the amount of their gift. If you have had five contacts before you ask, for example, you will get more money than if you had three contacts. Recall that one of our top ten measures on our Sustainable Funding Scorecard is that you must have at least two in-person or telephone contacts with each of your Multiple Year Giving Society Donors each year.

In other words, if you are ever going to develop a long-term relationship with your donors, you are going to need to stay in touch with them. Think of your lifelong friends and family—you have regular contact, sometimes hourly, daily, weekly, or annually. Even that annual holiday card from an old friend is enough to maintain a connection, especially if it is accompanied by a newsy "holiday letter" that engenders a newsy response from you. That natural personal contact—the give and take, back and forth dialog—is the golden nugget of cultivation. If the contacts are dry and impersonal and make your donor feel like a name or number on your donor list, then why bother? Conversely, just a small amount of effort, properly placed on those donors who have that deeper connection to your mission and who are nurtured gently over time, will produce wonderful ripened fruit, year after year.

CUSTOMIZING EACH CONTACT

People often ask: How many contacts does it take, and what does a contact look like? As you are seeing, the answer varies from donor to donor. The only way to know the right answer for each donor is to get to know that particular donor, step by step, contact by contact. It's as if you build the bridge one contact at a time, and it leads you naturally to the next step.

Once you view the cultivation process as ongoing for life, each "next Ask" would be nothing more than another natural contact at the perfect moment when the fruit is ripened. Instead of an ordeal to be dreaded, each Ask should be nothing more than a natural harvesting of ripened fruit.

And since there is no place in our model for random or superficial mass-contacts initiated by the organization, this approach should relieve you of a great deal of time-consuming mailing and party planning and allow you to focus on having a more customized dialog with each of your individual donors.

THE DEFINITION OF PERSONAL CONTACT

To create that customized dialog, each contact must be personal, according to our specific definition of the word. Let's dissect what we mean by personal and begin to turn it into a science. For a contact to qualify as personal in the Benevon Model, it needs to meet all five of these criteria:

1. One-on-one, speaking only to them, making each donor feel special.
It can't feel generic. It can't feel so standard and impersonal that the donor knows that this identical contact is being made with every other donor (even though that may be the case). Each communication has to be customized enough that the donor knows you are speaking only to them, and you know what they need to feel special.

Think about what your organization is currently doing to stay in contact with your donors. Most groups tell us that the majority of their time is spent in the least personal contacts—sending out the newsletter via bulk mail, the expensive printed invitations to which only a fraction of people respond, the formal thank-you letter which engenders no next contact, or the direct mail solicitation which keeps the relationship safely at arm's length.

Imagine if you were to take all the time and energy that your group puts into all those impersonal contacts and refocus on getting to know one subset of your donors and supporters personally, for example, your direct mail donors who give more than $500 per year, by cultivating them over time and then asking them for money, year after year. It would be far more satisfying to you and to the donors, and it would honor the mission of your organization, rather than demean it by entertaining, manipulating, and pressuring people to give long before the fruit has ripened.

Even if you didn't want to take the time to cultivate each of your donors one-by-one, face-to-face, you could at least begin with the people who have been dutifully giving—even small amounts—year after year, and begin to personalize those newsletters, invitations, and thank-you mailings to them, adding a hand-written note from someone who knows them and knows their particular interest in your organization. Again, the first element in our definition of "personal" is that each contact must *feel* personal—it can't be generic. It needs to be customized enough so that the donor knows you are speaking only to them. That is what will have each donor feel special. And sometimes it can be something as small—yet personal—as inquiring about their children or family.

2. Face-to-face, by phone, or by e-mail, so that the donor can respond right in the process of the contact.
There is no substitute for in-person, face-to-face communication. It allows for the immediate give-and-take we are looking for in a true dialog. It allows you to have eye contact, read body cues, and shake hands.

However, the simplest and most efficient form of cultivation contact is still a telephone call. Whether the purpose of the call is to inform, invite, ask, thank, or just to say hello, the telephone is second only to face-to-face in terms of allowing for a true dialog, letting you pick up voice inflection, pauses, hesitations, and subtle levels of interest.

Even if you don't reach the donor every time, once you get comfortable with leaving specific voicemail messages (the same way you do for friends and family members when you know they care enough to call you back), you will see the efficiency of these telephone contacts.

Consider this example: a few months before I stopped working at the school in Seattle where the model got started, a prominent board member asked if he could come and watch me work. He wanted to sit in my office and see what I did every day, in hopes of figuring out what more would be needed to keep the program going after I left.

Needless to say, I was not excited about the prospect of having someone sit in my tiny office, watching me talk on my telephone headset and put notes into a computer all day. Yet that was precisely what he did—for three days. At the end of the last day, he told me his conclusion: "I can see that if you had even more time in the day to just sit on the phone and make these calls, you would raise even more money!"

While this conclusion was a "no-brainer" to me, it was a huge "a-ha!" for this board member. He saw clearly the efficiency of the telephone as a medium for connecting with donors. He saw how readily the Point of Entry guests and subsequent donors wanted to talk to me when I called. He saw how important an impeccable database is for growing a major donor program.

At the next board meeting, he announced his generous offer—to fund three development positions, each for three years—tripling our "department" overnight!

My point: before you pick up the pen to write a letter, pick up the telephone. It is by far the most efficient form of personal contact for keeping this level of personal dialog going.

After face-to-face and telephone, e-mail is a close third. Not the blanket "spam" type of e-mails we all rush to delete. Rather, the more personal ones we reply to first. E-mail allows for immediate dialog and can be extremely personal if customized. While we don't naturally think of e-mail as "personal," if you look at the way we use it daily, it is extremely personal. It's almost embarrassing for me to admit that my close relationship with my eighty-nine-year-old mother-in-law is based largely on back and forth e-mail, nearly daily. It is an ideal medium that allows for her hearing loss and my travel schedule. We really are able to connect personally this way.

By way of example, after Hurricane Katrina, out of sheer desperation, many CEOs pulled out all the stops. Several we know of started sending out daily, and then weekly, e-mail updates to all of their prior donors. While these clearly were sent to a group of people and not to each donor individually, they were very personal letters, often written late at night by an exhausted CEO, seeking moral support from his own constituents, as much as anything. They were kind of an e-mail version of a narrative Wish List. While they never came out and asked for money outright, they clearly left the reader ready to write the check—and wanting to forward the e-mail on to others who could help fulfill some of the specific "Wish List" items needed.

3. Relevant to the donor's self-interest.

Focus each contact on whatever aspect of your program or service interests your donor most. For example, a health research organization could invite the donor to meet individually or in a group of donors with a research scientist who is working on the disease they have expressed a particular interest in. Conversely, stop sending out blanket invitations to events that are not of interest to all your donors and could be off-putting to them. As you get to know your donors well enough to anticipate their preferences and interests, you will know the natural next step they would like to take with you.

4. Timed to the donor's pace.

Each of us operates at our own pace, some faster, some slower. Thinking again of your friends and family, you know whose e-mails or phone calls you must reply to right away, versus those you can take a little longer to get back to. The same is true of your donors. Start by presuming that a one-week response time will be about right. As you learn each donor's unique pace, you can adjust this to be faster or slower.

5. Delivered via the donor's preferred medium.

This is very important in our world of rapid communication and personalization. Think of the many ways you have of communicating with your friends and family. You know which medium each person prefers. It may be more than one. Is it via phone or voicemail, e-mail, or in person? This will change over time as each donor's life circumstances change, often frequently. For example, the donor who wants you to call him on his boat over the holidays versus the CEO who wants you to e-mail her secretary to schedule your next call.

And don't forget the power of mixing the methods by which you communicate. While my mother-in-law and I enjoy frequent e-mail dialog, we also talk by phone once or twice a week, visit in person several times a year, and exchange written cards and letters.

SYSTEMATIZING THE CULTIVATION PROCESS

To turn all of this into a system—something you could leave as a legacy that would keep building towards sustainable funding for your organization—let's look at our Sample Master Cultivation Calendar on the next page and turn that into a Master Cultivation Calendar for your organization. You will need to make one of these for your organization and ultimately have each item on it tie to a to-do item on the personal calendar of one or more of your team members.

START WITH YOUR DONORS

Notice that down the left column are three broad categories of people you might want to cultivate: donors, volunteers, and staff. For the purposes of this discussion about donor cultivation, let's focus on that top category first: donors. You'll notice that each of the Multiple-Year Donor levels is listed separately. That is because we will be cultivating donors at each of these levels differently. Looking across the first row, in the month of January, you can see that the biggest donors (Sponsor a Classroom at $25,000 a year for five years) are taken to lunch by the executive director and board chair and then receive a one-on-one Follow-Up Call to tell them what action was taken on whatever was discussed at that lunch.

Donors at the Sponsor a Student level ($1,000 a year for five years) receive a personal thank-you call each January from the executive director or board chair. During that thank-you call, the caller will ask questions (from our Treasure Map Interview questions, included later in this chapter) and listen closely to the donor's response to learn which programs or issues are of most interest to each donor. Each call ends with a sincere thank you and a plan for the next contact, tracked in the donor tracking system with a "tickler" to pop up on the designated date.

These are precious donors. Likewise, the time of the executive director and board chair is extremely valuable, and your donors know this. Calls from high-level people within the organization mean a lot to the donors being called. These calls will show donors that they are truly appreciated.

SAMPLE MASTER CULTIVATION CALENDAR

Legend: ⊙ In Person ⊙ Mail ⊙ Online / ⊙ Phone ⊙ Fax

DONORS:	JANUARY	FEBRUARY	MARCH	APRIL	MAY	JUNE	JULY	AUGUST	SEPTEMBER	OCTOBER	NOVEMBER	DECEMBER
Sponsor a Classroom ($25,000/yr × 5 years) / Sponsor Ten Students ($10,000/yr × 5 years)	1 on 1 Lunch with E.D. and Board Chair / 1 on 1 Follow-Up with Past Requests	Donor-Hosted Points of Entry or Re-Entry		Spring Field Day	Classroom Sponsor Private Dinner	Pre-Graduation Reception		Board-Hosted Golf Day with Lunch		Classroom Sponsor Private Dinner	Telephone Follow-Up & Interviews	Added to be Table Captains Next Year
Sponsor a Student ($1,000/yr × 5 years)	Thank You Calls from E.D./Board Chair		Annual Report Mailed									Holiday Mailing to Non-Event Donors
$500 – $999	Post-holiday Thankathon / Invite to:					Graduation (Reserved Seats)	E.D. Site Visits / Special Summer Program	Summer Graduation		E.D. Site Visit		
$250 – $499												
$100 – $249												
<$100												

Newsletter ⊙⊙ — E-mail and Fax Updates Monthly (All Year)

Invite to free One-Hour Ask Event / Free One-Hour Ask Event ⊙⊙⊙⊙⊙

Back-to-School Open House/Curriculum Fair

VOLUNTEERS												
Current Board	Board Planning Retreat	Board/E.D. 1 on 1 Interviews										Board Recognition Dinner
Past Board								Nominating Committee 'Resolution' Calls				
Current Committee Members				1 on 1 Meetings with E.D.								
Tutors	Site Visit from E.D.		Thank You Calls from E.D.	Site Visit from E.D.	Volunteer Recognition Luncheon							
Mentors				Mentoring Program Dinner								
Computer Program Volunteers			Computer Night									
Music Program Volunteers		Winter Concert										

1 on 1 Notes and Birthday Cards from Supervisor (All Staff, All Year)

STAFF												
Main Office		Administrative Staff Retreat										All Staff Holiday Party
Program Staff			Program Staff Retreat		Staff Picnic							Holiday Gifts to Staff
Satellite Youth Program Staff												

As personal as these contacts may feel, they are still generic in the sense that there is a calendar telling us to contact donors at each level in a certain way at pre-set times each year. Some of the contacts are by mail, such as mailing the annual report to all donors in the month of March each year. Every possible "generic" contact you are already planning to have with your donors should go on this calendar, including inviting them to your gala, golf tournament, or Free Feel-Good Cultivation Events with a personal call or note even if you are using printed invitations.

To help you fill in the blanks for your particular donor levels, as we continue to discuss various donor categories, we have turned this into a Master Cultivation Calendar that you can make on your computer and customize for your organization. This time we have chosen different categories: Multiple-Year Donors, other donors, volunteers, and your Next Ten Asks.

Let's look at how you might cultivate the individuals in each of these categories.

CULTIVATING MULTIPLE-YEAR DONORS

Looking at the top category on the chart on the next page—Multiple-Year Donors—what are some of the cultivation activities you might have with these donors? This should include both individual and group cultivation activities. And remember, they must allow for give-and-take dialog, not just a one-way monologue.

Start by thinking of inspiring, mission-focused occasions within your organization—the times when you may have thought to yourself, *this is one of those moments that would be great for "outsiders" to see.*

Here are some examples of ways you can personally cultivate your Multiple-Year Donors:

- Call them to invite them to a special Free Feel-Good Cultivation Event.
- Invite them to meet a special researcher or art teacher.
- Call each donor to thank them for their gift.
- Have scholarship recipients call the donors to thank them.
- Invite the donor to lunch with their scholarship recipient.

MASTER CULTIVATION CALENDAR

		Jan	Feb	March	April	May	June	July	Aug	Sept	Oct	Nov	Dec
Multiple-Year Donors	$1K x 5 Years												
	$____ K x 5 Years												
	$____ K x 5 Years												
	One-time Ask Event Donors												
Other Donors	Large Annual Donors												
	Direct-mail Donors												
	Lapsed Donors												
Volunteers	Board and Former Board												
	Advisory or Development Committee												
	Special Event Volunteers												
Next Ten Asks	1												
	2												
	3												
	4												
	5												
	6												
	7												
	8												
	9												
	10												

- Invite top donors to be judges at a special mission-focused event like judging the booths at the job fair.
- Invite donors to conduct practice job interviews with low-income students looking for summer jobs.

Using these examples, you'll see other ways that you could fill in the blanks on the calendar for your Multiple-Year Donors.

CULTIVATING ONE-YEAR-AT-A-TIME DONORS

Going back to the Master Cultivation Calendar, let's look at the next level down—other donors who don't make pledges, but rather make one gift at a time. These are people who could potentially increase their gift or pledge quite easily. For example, these may be:

- People who attended your Ask Event and made a one-time gift as opposed to a multiple-year pledge.
- Larger annual donors (who may never have attended an Ask Event) who have supported you for one year or more.
- Direct mail donors.
- Prior ("lapsed") donors who have stopped giving.

The more you can segment each of these types of donors, the better. For example, you could segment them by the total amount of their prior giving and zero in on the categories you want to focus on cultivating first. Larger annual donors of, say, $500–$2,500 per year would certainly be a valuable category to cultivate.

You could cultivate them as a group by inviting them all to a special theater night or Free Feel-Good Cultivation Event where you showcase a graduate of the after-school sports program who has come back to give a lecture to the new kids. Just seeing the pride of the returning "success story" will remind donors of the long-term impact of your work—and of their gifts.

Don't forget to follow up with each attendee to get their feedback. Also, be sure to follow up with the people who couldn't attend—write to them, asking them to meet with you personally or come to your next group cultivation event.

Know-Thy-Donor

The main source of one-year-at-a-time donors for most groups is their existing direct-mail list. One of the first questions we ask when we start working with an organization is the obvious: "How many active donors do you have?" They can often proudly tell me a very large number, sometimes many thousands. Next question: "How many of those donors does someone here actually know?" This means someone has, at a minimum, talked to them in person or on the phone. Invariably, the answer to this question is: "Not many."

From time to time, we are called by progressive direct-mail companies to ask if we will work with their clients. "We've maxed out what we can do for them with mail. They've got to get to know these loyal, repeat direct-mail donors and grow them into major donors." They are right.

Most organizations do not need new donors. They already have plenty of existing donors. Rather than starting their cultivation system with a Point of Entry designed to introduce potential new donors to the organization, they need to start by getting to know their existing donors.

If you are serious about cultivation and want a quick, focused, personal way to connect with existing monthly or annual donors who are trying to tell you they care about you, I strongly encourage you to try our Know-Thy-Donor Program, even if just with a small subset of your donors.

Although we encourage first-year implementers of the model to use this method, they often do not get serious enough to actually consider it until their second year. I find that people tend to remember the name of this program, but they rarely actually do it!

Here's how it works:

Stratify Your Donors by Gift Level

Start your Know-Thy-Donor Program by getting your organization's real numbers. How many individual donors have given to you in the last two years? What is each donor's total gift for each of those years? You may be surprised to see how those $25-a-month checks add up, all from one loyal donor.

Now, classify the donors you have. How many give you, annually:

- $1,000 and above?
- $500–$999?
- $250–$499?
- $100–$249?

Don't be surprised to find some who give more than $10,000 a year without a personal contact from you.

What are they telling you with this gift? For whatever reason, they are believers in your work. They may have only a superficial understanding of the work of your organization, yet they give. Perhaps they had a family member with the disease you are working to eradicate. Maybe their mother or father received services from your organization many years ago.

If you are working to build a self-sustaining individual giving program that is based on one-on-one personal relationships, knowing more about each donor would be a great help. And there is only one way to find out—ask them!

Once you've analyzed the stratification of your existing donors, choose the cutoff level for your first round of calls. Let's say you decide to call all donors who give $500 or more a year and that you have 100 of them.

A High-Level Thank-a-Thon

The next step in your Know-Thy-Donor program is to enlist the support of a small group of your best and most passionate people—who also like talking on the telephone. It may be a mixed group of board, staff, and volunteers.

Before you give them the list of donors to be called and a recommended script, it is wise for the most senior development staff person or volunteer to make five or ten of these calls personally. That way you will get consistent feedback, all screened through the eyes and ears of the same caller. Based on what you learn in the first ten calls, you can then design a broader telephone survey which can be used by your team of callers.

When you are ready to put together a group of board and staff to phone these current donors personally, you can call it a thank-a-thon.

Once again, think of yourself as one of those loyal donors to your favorite organization. You have been giving faithfully for years, sending in checks in response to mail or phone appeals annually, quarterly, or monthly. Yet no one has ever called you to say thank you or to acknowledge your gift in person. It is a wonder you keep giving.

How should you start the calls? Yes, with a gracious and humble thank you. The main purpose of the call is to thank and appreciate the donor for their loyal support (and their recent gift if your timing is right). If you accomplish nothing else on this call, be sure they know how much you appreciate them.

Here is a suggested outline for the call:

Hello, Ms. _____. My name is _____. I'm on the board of_____. You've been a loyal supporter for several/many years, and we're calling to thank you. (Pause for response.) We are trying to gather input about what we could be doing better. Would you have a few minutes now for me to ask for your thoughts and advice?

Treasure Map Interview Questions

Then, slowly, ask three or four of the open-ended Treasure Map Interview questions listed here, noting the donor's answers along the way. The questions below are typical, but you should do your own work to come up with a list of questions that reflect what your organization wants to know.

1. What do you already know about our organization?
2. What images come to mind when you think of us?
3. How did you come to know about us or become involved with us?
4. What do you like about being a friend/supporter of our organization?
5. Where or how do you think we're really missing the boat?
6. What advice do you have for us?
7. What cues might we have missed from you?
8. How better could we be telling our story?
9. What could we be doing to involve more people?

Invite Them to a Point of Entry

Each call should end with an invitation to attend a Point of Entry or Point of Re-Entry (Free Feel-Good Cultivation Event) and to bring others if they would like. If they agree to attend, follow up with a confirmation card and a reconfirmation call the day before. Offer to provide them with transportation if necessary.

Your thank-a-thon calling team can do the phoning in a group one afternoon or evening. Or they can make their calls on their own from their home or workplace. Be sure their notes are put into your database tracking system. Imagine, for example, a team of five callers with each caller reaching five people a week. If you debrief well, you will have enough feedback to customize the next phase of the program.

I have seen board members get so excited about this that they recommend a Donor Services Representative Program or buddy system for pairing a volunteer or staff member with each donor above a certain dollar amount for two years. Imagine a donor who hears from someone at their favorite charity three or four times a year—including invitations to a variety of special Free Feel-Good Cultivation Events. When it is time for making an annual gift next year, they will be hard pressed to say no to a request for a larger gift. They may even feel connected enough to make a multiple-year pledge when asked, especially if it will be doubled by a matching gift Challenge Fund.

CULTIVATING VOLUNTEERS

Let's move now to the third level down on the Master Cultivation Calendar—your volunteers. Again, segment. Choose the three levels of volunteers you will focus on this year. Our calendar shows:

- Board and former board
- Advisory or development committee
- Special event volunteers

Think about what you are already doing to cultivate each of these groups. Your current and former board members are a very distinguished group, worthy of personal phone calls and individual face-to-face meetings once a year, whenever possible.

Former board members are often as passionate as ever about your work and happy to come back into service if there is a compelling need or project. In many cases, we have seen them as excellent team members on Benevon implementation teams because they are so committed to the organization's work of building towards sustainable funding.

What about your advisory committee or development committee members? What could you do to cultivate them? How about a special kick-the-tires Point of Entry for them to critique? Or you could invite them to your next Ask Event as VIP guests or table hosts for special tables of other VIP guests. Be sure to give them ribbons on their name badges to designate their special status.

I also like to see an annual face-to-face meeting with each of these committee members if possible. People truly appreciate that the executive director or top board member takes time to talk with them, update them on current issues at the organization, and ask for their input and advice—including who else they may know that might like to attend a Point of Entry.

So often, we see groups trying to cook up new special events just to show appreciation for volunteers like these. When you consider all the time and energy that goes into planning these events and then realize the disappointing turnout rates, you realize that time would be better spent in just picking up the phone and talking to each of these people, or in meeting with them one-on-one.

You will get a far greater quality of communication in these personal contacts. Just be sure to insert an emotional connection for people to the work of the organization, with a story or letter or testimonial of some type—something that shows this special volunteer that you know which program is most important to them.

MAKING CULTIVATION A SCIENCE

As you plot out your plan on the Master Cultivation Calendar, you will realize that it's time-consuming and can seem like a lot of work. That's because you are beginning to realize that cultivation is a science, not an art!

Remember our Sustainable Funding Scorecard measure: at least two in-person or telephone cultivation contacts with each Multiple-Year Donor per year (and, no, voicemail messages don't count). Of course this does not include all the other contacts you will be making all year, like Follow-Up Calls with Point of Entry guests, after events, etc.

How many Multiple-Year Donors does your organization have (people who have pledged to give at least $1,000 a year for five years)? Let's say you have thirty Multiple-Year Donors. That would mean you need to make a total of sixty contacts a year. Remember, these are people who are doing their best to tell you they love your work. They are not scary, distant strangers.

If you aimed to have one phone contact and one in-person contact each year, you could plan that out and accomplish it. Put the phone calls on your calendar. How would you plan to have the face-to-face contacts? At a Free Feel-Good Cultivation Event, at next year's Ask Event, or at a one-on-one lunch with your CEO and the donor? Put this all on your master calendar and then be sure it gets on someone's personal calendar on a particular date—not just on a to-do list.

Can you see that effective cultivation is a highly-refined numbers game? The number and type of contacts for each donor may vary based on their level of passion for your program, their own lifestyle and time constraints, and their wonderful and quirky personalities. You will become very familiar with these preferences as you get to know each donor over time.

As you weigh the time and effort of this customized cultivation approach against the more traditional mass-marketing approach, there is no question that the personal, focused approach is far more productive and satisfying, both for the donor and for you. If you keep listening to the donor, putting aside your own preferences about how you would want to be cultivated, you will find that your passionate donors practically cultivate themselves right through the Cultivation Superhighway, and they are ready and willing to give, when asked.

CHAPTER 9

CULTIVATING YOUR NEXT TEN ASKS

Now let's look at the final category on the Master Cultivation Calendar, the category we call the Next Ten Asks. If you are serious about implementing the model long-term, you will need an ever-current, rolling list of your next ten people to be asked for a gift over the next twelve months. The gift needs to be for a financial contribution at least as large as your lowest giving society level of $1,000 a year for five years.

Some groups have lists much longer than ten Asks in the next twelve months, which is fine. We find that ten is about the right number of potential major donors for a mid-sized nonprofit organization to be managing at any given time. So if your list is longer than ten, choose the first ten people to be asked; you can certainly keep adding more people and moving people up on the list as you complete each Ask.

If you have the staff and/or volunteer resources to cultivate and ask more than ten major donors a year, by all means make your list longer—just be realistic. We assume that if a name is on your list, that donor will be asked for that gift within the next twelve months.

To help you make up your list, here are a few suggestions of who to include:

- Existing Multiple-Year Donors who you feel have the commitment and capacity to give at higher levels.
- People who have come to your Point of Entry Events and other events but were unable to attend your Ask Event.
- People who attended but did not give at your Ask Event, yet you want to plan out a cultivation process for them.

- "Insiders" and "old-timers" like board members, former board members, and long-time volunteers, who may never have officially come to a Point of Entry or Ask Event, but you've been meaning to get around to asking them.
- Other smaller donors (via direct mail, Internet, or telephone) who you would like to cultivate toward a larger gift.
- People whose names have been on your radar for years, yet you have never gotten around to starting the cultivation process with them.

LEADERSHIP AND CHALLENGE GIFTS

At least two or three of your Next Ten Asks should be for a Leadership or Challenge Gift that can be announced at your next Ask Event. Remember, one of the three critical variables in growing the model is that you have a Leadership or Challenge Gift of increasing size each year that is announced at your Ask Event. After the first Ask Event, this is not optional.

One of the reasons we require a Leadership or Challenge Gift at the second year's Ask Event and beyond is to draw you into the major gifts cultivation and asking process. We want you to get as much experience in this as possible. You will learn just how natural this process can be when done properly. You will be cultivating until you know exactly when to ask and then asking for just the right amount.

Leadership Gift

As discussed previously, a Leadership Gift is a gift from one single donor or a pooled gift from a group of donors—including individuals, corporations, and foundations: for example, a pooled gift from your board members. To qualify as a true Leadership (or Challenge) Gift in our model, this is new money: not a gift you already had waiting in the wings or had already received. It is unrestricted money (like the money you will be raising at your Ask Event) intended to inspire others to give.

If we allowed groups to "count" contributions they already knew were coming as part of their Leadership (or Challenge) Gift, it would defeat the purpose of going out and asking for additional gifts. They would miss the chance to practice the natural flow of the whole process.

Challenge Gift

Like a Leadership Gift, which is essentially just a large, unrestricted gift or pool of gifts, a Challenge Gift may also come from one or more donors—but it will have some unique strings attached.

First, you'll need to decide what the Challenge Gift is being used to match. Perhaps it will match all gifts made on the day of the Ask Event, or all pledges of $1,000 or more, or even all the pledges over the next five years, dollar for dollar. Or perhaps it will match all gifts made at the Ask Event, two to one, meaning for every dollar someone gives at the Ask Event, the Challenge Gift will provide two dollars.

For Ask Event attendees who work for a company that has its own matching gifts program, their pledge of $1,000 a year for five years can be matched (in the two to one scenario) first by their company bringing it to $2,000 a year for five years ($10,000 total) and then doubled again, bringing it up to $20,000 total to the organization. That is a substantial incentive to a donor!

The best way to announce a Challenge Gift is to have the donor stand up and speak at your Ask Event, either just prior to the Pitch or by serving as the Pitch Person, saying, "My family and I are making this gift to challenge and inspire others to give generously to this wonderful organization." Either the donor or the Pitch Person needs to state very simply what will be matched. People will respond to that kind of sincerity and generosity.

Just be sure to clarify the "rules of the game" up front, including the expiration date on the challenge. Keep in mind that sometimes if the full amount of the challenge isn't used up, the donor(s) will give that money to the organization anyway—it's worth asking your Challenge Gift donors in advance how that scenario will be handled.

NEXT TEN ASKS

Let's go back to the Next Ten Asks. Here is a chart you should fill out with all the information about each Ask.

OUR NEXT TEN ASKS

Name	RL* (1-10)	Who Knows Them Best?	Asker(s)	Asking For	C/L?**	First Step and Date	Ask by When
1.							
2.							
3.							
4.							
5.							
6.							
7.							
8.							
9.							
10.							

* = Readiness level; ** = Challenge/Leadership Gift

Once you have your list of ten people, add them to the chart and begin filling out the rest of the chart.

Readiness Level

The second column, "RL," stands for "Readiness Level." We use a one through ten scale, with ten being the most ready.

You may be wondering how to determine the readiness level of a potential donor. If you think about it a bit, you'll realize you already have a fairly well developed radar for this. What are some of the signs people give to let you know they're getting ready to be asked?

1. They invite others to come to your events, such as Point of Entry Events.
2. They return your phone calls.
3. They answer your e-mails.
4. They ask for more information.
5. They ask questions.
6. They give you ideas and advice.
7. They volunteer, offer their time, show up, and help out.
8. They start talking about "we."
9. They tell others about you and refer others, especially family and close friends who they trust.
10. They make in-kind gifts of goods and services.

Trust your instincts. If you suspect that it might be too early, wait. Perhaps it's been awhile since someone from your organization has had personal contact with this donor. It might seem a bit forward to move right to asking them for money during your next meeting or visit. Have another contact to ripen the fruit, and wait until you are sure the person is ready to be asked.

At a recent Benevon 301 Workshop, one of the groups in our Five-Year Sustainable Funding Program filled out this Next Ten Asks chart. We were amazed to see that they had nearly thirty names on the list, all rated at a ten level of readiness!

When I asked them why they hadn't already made the Asks, they hesitated. We talked through several of the donor situations, and we all realized that, while these donors definitely will give when asked, they were each more realistically at a seven to nine readiness level, not a ten. By stepping back and designing the next cultivation contact for each of these donors, they were able to time each Ask perfectly and maximize each gift.

Then there is the other end of the spectrum, where you have people on your list who are just a two or three readiness level. That is fine; do not rush the process. Tell the truth and rank them as two or three, and begin cultivating them to become a ten.

As you tune your radar up for readiness level, you will become more and more comfortable with the cultivation and asking process.

You'll start to see that any hesitation you may have about asking should be regarded as an opportunity for another cultivation contact.

Who Knows Them Best?

Decide with your team which person or people from your organization know each potential donor the best. These are the people who will be involved in cultivating these donors to move them up to a level ten readiness and who may be involved in the eventual Asks. Even if these people who know the donors best won't be directly involved in the cultivation process, they will have advice about the donors' situations and unique preferences.

Who Will Ask?

Your asker or askers should be people who have been involved in the cultivation process and who the potential donors know and respect. Ideally at least one of the askers is at a peer level of stature or wealth in the community and is well-linked to your organization, preferably a board member. If there will only be one asker, it must be this person. Many groups prefer two askers. That way, the executive director or development director can back up the volunteer with facts about the program and answer questions that the volunteer may be uncomfortable answering.

Asking For What?

It's important to determine early in the process just what you want to ask these people for. This is the only way you will really be able to know their readiness levels, since their readiness levels will vary depending on what you may be asking for. As you cultivate these donors, you will be able to judge what would be appropriate to ask for and you can adjust your goal accordingly.

Much has been written about how to gauge a donor's capacity to give—a percentage of their assets, a multiple of their past annual giving, etc. We work with our groups to take into consideration several factors, such as past giving, level of interest in the organization, and appropriate step up to the next level. We look at this gift as an interim gift—not the ultimate gift you will ever get from this donor. So the amount you ask for needs to make sense to the donor. For example, if the donor is a member of your giving society at $1,000 a year for five years, the next Ask might be for the next level up in your giving society or the highest level of, say, $25,000 a year for five years. If this gift is part of a major gifts, capital, or endowment campaign, you may want to increase the Ask.

Ultimately, when determining the amount to ask for, we encourage our groups to ask themselves: *Will we feel good about the donor saying yes to this amount? Will the donor feel good about saying yes to that amount?* At the end of each Ask, the donor should feel so good about it that they look forward to talking with you again—and being asked again for more.

We view asking as merely one more contact on a continuous Cultivation Superhighway. In fact, as soon as each Ask is complete, we begin the next round of cultivation and involvement, leading up to another Ask with this same donor.

First Step, Date, and By When?

Now, decide what the first step in moving this person toward the Ask is, and give that step a specific date: lunch with board chair and executive director by January 10, invite to our Point of Entry by July 15, etc.

You will also need to give yourselves a deadline for when you will have completed this Ask. Everything that happens between the first step and Ask date will be mapped out on a cultivation plan for this person.

CUSTOMIZED CULTIVATION

Once you have your list of Next Ten Asks, the cultivation process becomes a lot more real. Although you will map out your best prediction of a step-by-step cultivation plan, since you are dealing with real people, the actual cultivation process may not always unfold exactly according to your plan.

Here is an example of how this process can play out, if you let the fruit ripen naturally:

Meet Don and Elizabeth

October 1: Don attends a Point of Entry Event for Great Kids After-School Center, having been referred by a colleague in his consulting firm. He meets the director, and he hears a staff member tell a story of a twelve-year-old boy who finished high school thanks to this program. Don is given a brochure, a Fact Sheet, and a Wish List to take home.

October 4: Don receives a Follow-Up Call three days later from the development director. Don requests more information about the math tutoring program; he also refers his wife to attend a future Point of Entry.

October 11: The development director sends Don information about the math tutoring program with a handwritten cover letter. The letter ends with, "I'll give you a call in a week or so to answer any further questions you may have. Thank you again for encouraging your wife to come and visit our program."

In the meantime, Don's wife, Elizabeth, is contacted and invited to a Point of Entry, at the recommendation of her husband. Several potential tour dates are offered. She agrees to attend in two weeks.

October 18: The development director calls Don to follow up on the material mailed. Don has only had a chance to glance at the material, yet seems apologetic and genuinely interested. The development director suggests a meeting with Don and the head of the math tutors in two weeks. She arranges a time that will be easy for Don and convenient for the staff person as well. Don promises to read the materials before the meeting.

October 22: Don's wife, Elizabeth, attends a Point of Entry with one of her law firm colleagues, Sheila. Elizabeth immediately connects with the arts program, and Sheila is touched as she observes a young child being tutored to read. Both women leave the tour saying they would like to think more about what they have seen and how they might like to get involved. The development director says she will call them in a few days.

October 29: Don comes back to meet with the math tutor coordinator. The coordinator explains in-depth the After-School Center's system for teaching math, then gives several examples of how this system has been adapted to students at different skill levels. His dedication and commitment are palpable. Don is visibly moved in the meeting. He asks what this program needs to be more successful, mentioning the computers he saw listed on the Wish List.

By December, Don and Elizabeth have been back to visit three times. They have donated two computers and arranged a meeting for the executive director with a friend who owns an office supply store. Elizabeth's law colleague, Sheila, has arranged for their law firm employees to volunteer over the holidays as their annual community service project.

By March, the After-School Center has taken a Point of Entry "on the road" to Sheila and Elizabeth's law firm for a lunch presentation, as well as to Don's consulting firm. Each person who has expressed interest has been followed up with personally in much the same way as Don has been.

By June, Don, Elizabeth, and Sheila have been invited to become Table Captains at the fall Free One-Hour Ask Event for the After-School Center. They are delighted to accept. They make their lists of guests to sit at their tables and begin inviting these friends to attend Point of Entry Events at the after-school site.

At the Ask Event in September, Don, Elizabeth, and Sheila make their first gifts. Don and Elizabeth pledge $10,000 a year for each of the next five years to sponsor a class of after-school students. Sheila pledges $1,000 a year for five years to sponsor a student. Of the remaining twenty-seven guests at their collective tables, over $60,000 more is pledged. Friends leave the event inspired, thanking Don, Elizabeth, and Sheila for inviting them. Several indicate they would like to become Table Captains themselves at next year's event.

Three years later: Elizabeth has joined the board of the After-School Center and, through her vast contacts alone, has brought tremendous resources to the organization. Don personally tutors a math student and has helped the organization find a new building to accommodate its expanded programs and student population. Don has offered to co-chair the capital campaign committee, and he and Elizabeth have discussed the size of their Leadership Gift. Sheila's church group has adopted the After-School Center as has her son's high school class.

And so it goes, the Cultivation Superhighway, an ever-deepening series of personal, relevant, and timely contacts.

FOOTBALL FIELDS

Now, let's go back and dissect this personal cultivation process a bit further and turn it into a cultivation template called the Next Steps to a Yes form, which we affectionately refer to as the "football field."

NEXT STEPS TO A YES

Person to be asked: _____ Asking for: _____ Cultivation Coordinator: _____		Goal	
		Date	Desired Outcome
10.			
9.			
8.			
7.			
6.			
5.			
4.			
3.			
2.			
1.			

Pretend that you are down at the bottom of the football field at step one (the ten-yard line) with a potential donor, Don, and your goal is a gift of $10,000 a year for five years. You can see how we might have filled in the football field chart. Yet many of those twists and turns were unpredictable. How could we have known that Don's wife Elizabeth would have become involved, let alone that she would involve her law firm and that her colleague Sheila would have gotten so involved?

While it's true that there's no way to precisely anticipate each step along the way, it is important to write out a possible scenario of how the process could go and then tweak and modify it as you go. We have found that without thinking through the full football field scenario, groups often plow ahead with donors who are barely interested in their cause, wasting everyone's time and alienating donors.

The Don and Elizabeth scenario took nearly a year until they made their first gift. All of the groundwork had been laid for them to engage many others and for them to remain engaged in the organization long-term.

Like growing the most delicious fruit, the process cannot be rushed. It will take precisely as long as it needs to take. For some donors, the process is very quick, merely a matter of a few weeks. For others, it may take months or years. In our model, we allow six to nine months for the cultivation and asking process, just as a rule of thumb. For larger gifts, it may take longer.

Be sure to put the name of the person responsible for the overall process for each donor and the dates by when the first three steps will happen so that these dates can be added to the bottom section of the Master Cultivation Calendar: Next Ten Asks. Ultimately, each item on this master calendar will be entered into your tracking system and into the personal calendar of the person accountable for the cultivation of that donor.

CHAPTER 10

THREE SAMPLE FOOTBALL FIELDS

Let's look at three different football field scenarios. The first is for a couple who have already given to your Multiple-Year Giving Society and you would like to ask them for a Challenge or Leadership Gift. The second is for a new potential donor who has been to a Point of Entry but not been cultivated further. And the third is for a couple who you would love to get to know, but as of now, they aren't even on your football field—in fact, they are barely out in the parking lot! Having these three templates will give you a good sense of the breadth and pace of the process.

Example One: Richard and Louise

Richard and Louise are parents of a forty-year-old son, Jeffrey, who has a moderate developmental disability and lives in a group home run by the Care Center. The family has been involved with the Care Center since Jeffrey was a child, making annual gifts of $100 or less in response to the holiday mailing. They attend a Free Feel-Good Cultivation Event—the community dinner—where many of the residents in the Care Center's multiple group homes prepare a recognition dinner for their families. They share stories of what they have learned over the years, living and working in the community.

The Care Center's development director, Diligent Dee Dee, makes the Five-Step Follow-Up Call after the Free Feel-Good Cultivation Event and asks, "Is there any other way you could see yourself becoming involved with us?" Richard and Louise respond, "Just tell us how else we can help!" Dee Dee tells them about the upcoming Ask Event and invites them to become Table Captains. They each say yes—meaning they agree to host two tables!

Richard and Louise love the Ask Event. Each of them joins the giving society at $1,000 a year for five years, and they make their first payments that day. Their tables are full, and their guests give generously.

Although it's been only six months since the Ask Event, the Care Center is planning next year's Ask Event, carefully considering who might make a Leadership or Challenge Gift to be announced at the second Ask Event, and Richard and Louise seem like they might be ready to step up—even this soon after making their first pledge.

What might the cultivation process look like?

First of all, how would we rank them on readiness level? Maybe somewhere in the seven to eight range, in terms of how connected they feel to the organization. While sensing they could be a "ten" soon, the Care Center doesn't feel ready to call and schedule the meeting to ask for the gift.

What might be a natural next contact (the first step on this football field)?

Let's look at what transpires with them after the Ask Event.

The day after the Ask Event, Diligent Dee Dee calls to thank both Richard and Louise, individually. Louise is gushing with praise about the event—how much it honored the people served by the organization and how it really connected the audience with something she has been living with for so long. "You really put a human face on such a big, scary label. My friends were so moved, they left thanking me for inviting them! Several of them asked to be invited to my table again next year—of course you haven't asked me yet, but yes, Richard and I would both love to do it again."

Diligent Dee Dee, gushing in return, thanks Louise sincerely for what she and Richard added to the event—their deep personal connection to the mission, so graciously hosting two tables and, of course, giving so generously themselves. Dee Dee goes on to ask if anyone at Louise's table mentioned anything else as they were leaving the Ask Event. She highlights the four guests who did not turn in their pledge cards and the one guest, Candace, who checked the box marked, "Please contact me. I have other thoughts to share." Being good friends of Louise's, each of these guests spoke with her before they left the event. Three of her friends said they wanted to talk with their husbands before deciding what to give. One said she really loved the event, but was already so involved with her own son's school, she wasn't in a position to give financially at this time. And the woman who had checked off the "Please contact me" box said she wanted to talk with her family's foundation to see if they might be able to give at the highest level, $25,000 for five years! "If I had known more about this wonderful organization, we would have been giving here long ago," she said.

Diligent Dee Dee, not one to deviate from the model, asks if Louise would like her to contact Candace. Louise says, "You know, I was thinking of inviting her to one of the tours you're doing now, so she can really see what we're doing up close. How about if I give her a call and tell her you'll be contacting her next week to invite her to a tour? I would love to come with her that day if there's anything I could add to help 'seal the deal.'"

Two weeks later, Louise and her friend Candace attend a Point of Entry Event, and they stay later for a prearranged private meeting. Now Candace is prepared to give. She has already gotten the approval from her family foundation to make the gift of $25,000 a year for five years, and everything she has heard and seen at the Point of Entry confirms how happy she is to make the gift.

Louise is moved to tears at the meeting, thanking Candace for her generosity. Diligent Dee Dee does her homework, thanking Louise again next day, this time asking if Louise and Richard might be willing to host a private Point of Entry for some of their table guests, since many of them now have told Louise that their spouses want to learn more about the organization as well.

Five months after the first Ask Event, this private mid-morning Point of Entry takes place, moving everyone to tears, largely thanks to the Visionary Leader Talk and Richard's own personal testimonial and expression of gratitude to the Care Center for all they have done for their family over the years. Richard and Louise end with an enthusiastic invitation to any of the Point of Entry guests to join them again at their respective tables at the second Ask Event.

Diligent Dee Dee has been doing a brilliant job! In addition to closing the loop on the five non-givers at Louise's Ask Event table, she is cultivating Louise and Richard, very naturally, towards a Leadership or Challenge Gift to be announced at the second Ask Event.

Three months before the Ask Event, Dee Dee feels they are ready to be asked. She would like them to give $10,000 a year for five years, in addition to paying off their current pledges, year-by-year!

While Richard and Louise know a few of the Care Center's board members, Dee Dee and the Care Center's CEO feel they want to make this Ask themselves. Dee Dee calls to ask Louise if the four of them can meet for lunch soon, saying, "We have something special we want to talk about with you."

The Ask goes well. Richard and Louise are truly thrilled to say yes to making the Care Center's first Leadership Gift to be announced at the Ask Event. They modestly ask to remain anonymous but Dee Dee, knowing them well now, prevails by convincing them to let their name be used "to inspire others to do the same thing" and to stand and be recognized when the gift is announced at the event.

At the second year's Ask Event, Richard and Louise are back, each hosting a table again. This time, three of the guests at each table are friends who came last year and did not give. Since they attended the private Point of Entry Event and have been followed up with, they all make gifts this year. Two guests per table were prior donors at the first Ask Event. One pays off the second year's installment at the Ask Event. The other, inspired by the announcement of Richard and Louise's Leadership Gift, pays off his prior pledge in full and makes a new pledge at the next highest level in the Multiple-Year Giving Society. The remaining five guests at each table are new people. Those who attended a prior Point of Entry (two at each table) make a gift. The remaining three people at each table do not give, but one says, "Please contact me. I have other thoughts to share."

Richard and Louise are honored to have their gift announced at the event. The overall results of the event increase by 30%, not counting the generous Leadership Gift from Richard and Louise.

Louise offers to host a dinner party in their home for all members of the giving society's top two levels ($10,000 and $25,000 a year for five years) two months later. At the end of the evening, the board chair, who is also a giving society member, invites Louise to join the Care Center's board. Louise graciously accepts, with Richard's blessing.

Here's how the football field for Richard and Louise might look:

NEXT STEPS TO A YES

Person to be asked: ___Richard and Louise___
Asking for: ___$10,000 x 5 years___   **$10,000 x 5**
Cultivation Coordinator: ___Dee Dee___

	Date
10. Richard and Louise host a Free Feel-Good Cultivation Event in their home for top two levels of society donors. Louise agrees to join Board of Directors.	Jan 15; Year 3
9. Richard and Louise host tables again at second Ask Event, where their Leadership Gift is announced; their guests give generously.	Nov 11; Year 2
8. Dee Dee and Care Center director ask Richard and Louise for a Leadership Gift of $10,000 x 5 years. They say yes and agree to be recognized at the Ask Event to inspire others to give.	Aug 10; Year 2
7. Richard and Louise host a private Point of Entry. Richard gives a testimonial, and they invite guests to next year's Ask Event.	April 7; Year 2
6. Dee Dee follows up with Candace. Louise and Richard agree to host a private Point of Entry for their Ask Event guests and friends.	Nov 26; Year 1
5. Candace attends a Point of Entry with Louise. She meets afterward and gives $25,000 x 5 from her family foundation.	Nov 25; Year 1
4. Dee Dee has Five-Step Follow-Up Call with Louise and reviews status of non-givers, including Candace, who has a family foundation. Louise offers to invite Candace to a Point of Entry.	Nov 11; Year 1
3. Richard and Louise host two tables at Ask Event. Each joins the Multiple-Year Giving Society at the $1,000 x 5 level.	Nov 10; Year 1
2. Five-Step Follow-Up Call; Richard and Louise agree to host two tables at the Ask Event.	Sept 13; Year 1
1. Free Feel-Good Cultivation Event community dinner.	Sept 10; Year 1

What do you notice about the process of cultivation from this example of Richard and Louise?

Do you notice how easily and naturally the whole process seemed to flow? That's because Louise and Richard were truly passionate about the work of the Care Center. It wasn't an obligation to them. It was part of their mission in the world. Giving to the Care Center was part of the larger legacy they plan to leave. In fact, you can see how naturally they could be cultivated further after this scenario to give more for the next expansion of the Care Center's facilities or towards the endowment fund the Care Center aims to build over the next seven to ten years. Since Jeffrey is their only child, they may make a planned gift, including both Jeffrey and the Care Center in their planning.

And what about Diligent Dee Dee? Did you notice how she just seemed to be there at the right moment, doing her job? She never seemed to be rushing the process or pushing too hard. That's because she was listening so closely to her donors and taking their cues for the next step. She trusted the natural, "fruit-ripening" process of the model, always letting the donors proceed at their own pace—which, in this case, was fast!

Example Two: Nancy

Let's move on to a second example, of Nancy, who is on the Next Ten Asks list for the Teen Suicide Hotline, but, to date, has only attended a Point of Entry. What might the football field for Nancy look like?

Nancy came to a Point of Entry at the invitation of her closest friend, Carol, whose daughter, Lisa, had been having a hard time coping with depression. Lisa—now a senior in high school and doing well—had a very rough time during her middle school years, when she had called into the Hotline on several occasions for support. Carol hadn't even known that such a service existed and was eternally grateful for the tangible support they offered, including a list of therapists, one of whom "worked" for Lisa. The whole experience of teen depression and the alarming rates of teen suicide were real eye-openers for Carol, a single mom, and she felt a strong need to give back and to help other parents in similar situations.

Nancy loved the Point of Entry, and when she received the Fol-low-Up Call from the Hotline's Diligent Dee Dee, she readily jumped in and said that she would like to become more involved, but she was so busy with her work as a real estate broker, she didn't know that she could actually do much to help. She asked Dee Dee to call her back in two months, after her busy season at work had passed. Of course, Carol, a Table Captain at the Hotline's spring Ask Event, invited Nancy to sit at her table. Nancy said yes but, in the end, couldn't make it.

Now, two months after Nancy attended the Point of Entry, Dee Dee wonders how to get back on Nancy's radar, since the Hotline wants to ask her for a gift of $1,000 a year for five years. But it seems too soon to do that. Dee Dee has rated Nancy a four on the readiness scale, sensing Nancy's deeper commitment to the Hotline's mission and her loyalty to Carol and Lisa. But there is more work to be done. What might the next steps look like?

Dee Dee's trusty database tracking system reminds her to call Nancy two months after she attended the Point of Entry. In the call, Dee Dee again thanks Nancy for coming and asks what Nancy thought of the Point of Entry. Nancy immediately mentions how impressed she was by seeing how young the Hotline volunteers are in the Peer Hotline program. That said to Nancy that these "kids" understood the depth of the problem and were willing to go through the Hotline's rigorous volunteer program to learn to deal with life-and-death situations, 24/7. "Truly," Nancy tells Dee Dee, "if those peer volunteers hadn't been there, Carol's daughter Lisa may not have made it."

When Dee Dee asks, "Is there any way you could see yourself becoming involved with us?" Nancy replies, "You know how much I would love to help you, but I am just so busy with work. Just keep me on your list, keep inviting me to your events, and I will do my best to make it to one of them soon."

Dee Dee finally asks, "Is there anyone else you can think of who we ought to invite to a Hotline tour?" This question perks Nancy up. "You know, you just reminded me, when I was there on the tour, I had a thought that my real estate women's group might like to take on something like this. We have monthly lunch meetings. Do you ever provide speakers?"

"Yes," Dee Dee replies, "we certainly could arrange to have our executive director, Ron, come out to speak to your group. But let me suggest one more idea: we offer private Hotline tours for community groups. Would you like to arrange to have your women's group meet here together and take the tour?" Nancy replies, "Maybe later down the road, but for now, let's start with the lunch speaker."

Over the next few weeks, Dee Dee arranges the logistics for Ron's lunch talk, making sure it includes several stories interwoven with some of the shocking statistics about teen suicide, right there in the community. The luncheon goes very well. Nancy introduces Ron as the speaker, tactfully weaving in her personal connection to the Hotline's work, and encouraging anyone interested after today to take the Point of Entry tour. Of course, the guests are moved to tears. Several of them come up to Ron and Nancy at the end of the program, sharing personal stories of teenagers in their lives who have been touched by this issue.

Dee Dee gives Nancy five days to digest all the feedback after the lunch talk, then calls her to follow up. Nancy tells Dee Dee about all the positive comments she has received, and says that she would like to host a private Point of Entry at the Hotline's offices next month.

Eleven people show up for the Point of Entry, and Nancy is delighted. She has also invited Carol to be there, who has offered to come forward and do a short testimonial at the end of the Point of Entry. While it is still a sensitive subject for her, she wants others to know that there is hope—that with proper intervention, teenagers can turn their lives around.

The Point of Entry is very powerful. Like Nancy, many of the guests are surprised to see how young the Hotline call center volunteers are. Dee Dee—the tour guide—highlights the rigorous, seventy-two-hour training program each volunteer must complete, being observed on twelve hours of phone calls, and tested on a list of over 300 community resources for referral. Carol's testimonial is straight from the heart—a mom who loves her teenage daughter but truly didn't know where to turn. "If it weren't for this place, I don't believe I would have my beautiful daughter with me right now. They saved her life."

In addition to the eleven guests who are now out spreading the word about this amazing Teen Hotline, Nancy is becoming more and more engaged.

Dee Dee follows up to thank her and get her feedback on the private Point of Entry. "They all loved it," Nancy reports. "And I had my own 'a-ha!' moment, sitting there, listening to Carol's story about Lisa again and seeing those teen volunteers. I really do want to become more involved with the Hotline, and I felt badly that I didn't make it to that fundraising breakfast Carol invited me to. Tell me more about what you need."

Right there on the phone, without missing a beat, Diligent Dee Dee says, "You know, we launched our Lifeline Society at that breakfast, where people pledge to give $1,000 a year for five years and make their first payment that day. It would be wonderful if you could join us at that level and come to the breakfast next year. In fact, given the responses I'm hearing from your friends who came to the tour last week, you might want to consider becoming a Table Captain for your own table of ten people. We could seat you all right next to Carol's table."

"That sounds great! I'd love to do both of those things. Why don't you give me the date for the breakfast right now so I can get it on my calendar early!"

And so the process goes on.

For the people on your Next Ten Asks list, you might only have enough information to write down the next two or three steps. Be sure to put your next steps and their anticipated dates. This will give you enough of a pathway to keep moving. You can always tweak as you go along to allow for the many curves and deviations along the way. Often those deviations become the start of a new football field for someone else who entered the picture. And as you move through each step, the pathway will become clearer for the next few possible steps after that. Finally, there is no need to use up all ten steps on the football field diagram provided here. For some donors, two or three steps will be enough. For others, you may need ten steps or more.

Nancy's football field might look something like this:

NEXT STEPS TO A YES

Person to be asked: _____ Nancy _____ Asking for: _____ $1,000 x 5 years _____ Cultivation Coordinator: _____ Dee Dee _____	$1,000 x 5

		Date
10.		
9.		
8.		
7.	Nancy hosts a table at the Ask Event with many friends who have attended Point of Entry Events and been cultivated. Four join the Lifeline Society.	Nov; Year 1
6.	Dee Dee follows up with Nancy. Nancy is inspired and asks how she can help. Dee Dee asks Nancy to join Lifeline Society ($1,000 for five years) and to be a Table Captain at the Ask Event.	Aug; Year 1
5.	Nancy hosts a Point of Entry for eleven guests; Carol gives a testimonial.	Aug; Year 1
4.	Dee Dee follows up with Nancy, who offers to host a private Point of Entry Event.	July; Year 1
3.	Executive director speaks to Nancy's real estate group — Nancy introduces him there. Many guests want to go to a Point of Entry Event.	July; Year 1
2.	Dee Dee follows up again (by phone). Nancy requests a speaker for her real estate women's group. Dee Dee offers a private Point of Entry for them. Nancy prefers speaker only.	May; Year 1
1.	Nancy attends a Point of Entry. In her Follow-Up Call, she requests to be called back in two months. She misses the Ask Event because she's too busy.	March; Year 1

Example Three: Marty and Pam

For our final example, let's take someone off the Next Ten Asks for a Christian school: Martin Smith, who is not yet familiar with the school. Martin is a big-name person in town—an entrepreneur who has made a large amount of money in real estate development. He is recently married, has no children, and is a person of strong Christian faith. In terms of readiness level, Martin is not even on the football field. Yet Dee Dee has reason to believe he would give when asked, if the proper cultivation work were done first. The school's ultimate goal is to have their new building paid for and named after Martin's family—a $1.5 million gift.

The place to start is with finding what we call "the connector person." Dee Dee starts by looking at the school's current Treasure Map to see who may know Martin well enough to invite him to a Point of Entry. Has that potential connector person ever attended a Point of Entry? If not, who could invite him to attend one?

Dee Dee asks around and finds that, lo and behold, the board chairman, Bob, knows Martin from a networking group of Christian businessmen. Also, Bob's wife and Martin's wife, Pam, are in the same Bible study group. While Bob's three kids are grown now, they are all alumni of the school. Bob and his wife are considerably older than Martin, but Bob is very well respected in the Christian community and could certainly make a call to Martin to invite him to a Point of Entry.

Sure enough, Martin accepts. He and Pam have been looking to get more involved in something in the community, they've heard good things about the school, and, Martin confesses, they are in the process of adopting a child, so Christian education is something that is very much on their minds these days.

Bob proposes a private Point of Entry for Martin and Pam together, where the headmaster will speak about the history of the school and his vision for moving forward, along with a tour of the school, clearly showing the need for a larger building.

Pam and Martin (by now, Dee Dee knows him as "Marty") are extremely impressed with the school's rigorous academic programs. Being a former college track star, Marty is impressed to see the playing fields and regulation-size track and how well the field is maintained. He also enjoys meeting the athletics director during one stop on their Point of Entry tour. Pam is drawn in by the music program, having sung in a church choir all her life.

By now you can probably fill in the blanks on the football field for some of the other possible scenarios. Over time, if properly cultivated, you can see that Martin and Pam could easily become more involved, coming to Ask Events, hosting tables, coming to Free Feel-Good Cultivation Events, hosting parties in their home, joining the board of directors or the capital campaign committee, and making that first lead gift of $1.5 million. Eventually, they could establish a named family endowment at the school as part of a larger endowment campaign. The next page includes an example of how the football field for Marty and Pam might look.

NEXT STEPS TO A YES

Person to be asked: Marty and Pam

Asking for: Leadership Gift of $1.5 million

Cultivation Coordinator: Dee Dee

$1.5 M

	Date
10. Marty joins the board of directors after the successful completion of capital campaign. He envisions a large endowment fund and works to fulfill it.	Sept; Year 2
9. Marty and Pam say yes to a $1.5 million gift ($300,000 x 5 years) while continuing to give $10,000 a year to the Multiple-Year Giving Society. Marty agrees to chair the capital campaign and is involved in the cultivation process for several other Christian businessmen who are potential donors.	May; Year 2
8. The board chair and headmaster meet with Marty to ask him to chair the campaign committee. They ask him to consider a lead gift and say they would love to name the building after him and his family. Marty wants to discuss with Pam first and asks for a Follow-Up Call in one week.	April; Year 2
7. The headmaster invites Marty to attend a planning lunch with seven prominent local Christian businessmen to discuss leadership for the upcoming capital campaign and lays out an $8 million plan for major expansion including a new middle school, gymnasium, and music rooms. Marty and Pam adopt their baby girl. The school sends a lovely baby gift.	Feb; Year 2
6. Marty and Pam attend the Free Feel-Good Cultivation Event which includes a short program from the headmaster and a prominent Christian speaker, reminding people of the school's larger mission.	Jan; Year 2
5. Dee Dee follows up and invites Marty and Pam to a "high-end" private Free Feel-Good Cultivation Event at the home of another big donor.	Dec; Year 1
4. "Marty" and Pam co-host a table at the Ask Event; they join Multi-Year Giving Society at the $10,000 x 5 level.	Nov; Year 1
3. Dee Dee invites Pam back to meet with the music teacher and Martin to meet with the athletics director. The headmaster is there to greet them each time.	June; Year 1
2. Dee Dee follows up and learns that Martin loves the athletics program, while Pam loves the music program.	May; Year 1
1. Bob invites Martin and Pam to a Point of Entry, which includes several inspiring student and parent testimonials and lots of stories.	April; Year 1

Now that you have seen the football field process in action, it is your turn to write out a football field scenario for each of your Next Ten Asks.

CHAPTER 11

ASKING NATURALLY

DONOR READINESS

There is a point, as you can feel yourself approaching the end of each football field, where it is time to evaluate the donor's readiness and decide whether it truly is the right time to ask. The easiest way to know if you are ready to ask is if you can answer all of these pre-Ask questions before each and every personal Ask you make. Do not guess at your answers. If you don't honestly know the answer, it is a good sign that you may need to complete more cultivation contacts before asking. It's far better to take the time to have another one or two personalized contacts, than to rush into the Ask prematurely, risking alienating your donors, after all the good work you have been doing.

Can you answer each of these questions for your donor?

Pre-ask Questionnaire

1. *Exactly who will be asked?*

   Have you cultivated all of the key decision-makers? Should spouses, partners, children, parents, or business partners be included? Including them in the asking meeting or call tells them you respect their "vote" in the process. Down the road, one of these other people may become your main donor.

2. *Who will do the asking?*

   Will it be one person or more? Are these the people most appropriate to be asking this particular donor? Would another board member enhance the asking team? Is the asker too closely connected to the donor? Would a slightly more distant asker be better? Who is this donor's favorite person at the organization? Looking from the donor's self-interest, by whom would they be most flattered to be asked? To whom could this person only say yes?

3. *Exactly what will be asked for?*

It's fine for the Ask to include more than one component: to make a Leadership Gift to the Sponsor-an-Artist Fund, as well as to co-chair the annual event or be a regional campaign chair. This tells the donors you are looking for a longer-term relationship. They are valued for their many talents and resources, not just their money.

4. *Where will the Ask take place?*

Ideally, would it be at a restaurant, a home, or an office? Are you prepared for it to happen spontaneously at another location that may be more convenient for the donor?

5. *What is the bottom-line result you will come away with?*

It is good to have a range of Asks, starting with the biggest, then scaling back to the bottom line. It is often helpful to include items other than money in what you are asking for.

6. *What makes you think this person is ready to be asked now?*

Have there been any recent cues? Have you hinted to the donor that you will be asking for their support soon? Keep putting yourself in the donor's shoes. Will they feel comfortable and receptive to an Ask now?

7. *What are your biggest concerns, fears, and reasons for procrastinating in making this Ask?*

Don't be embarrassed to list even seemingly trivial things. Often these are legitimate, especially if they concern donor-readiness.

8. *Does the person have an abundance of what you are asking for?*

If you don't know or are unsure, how could you find out? Who could you ask? Remember, donors want to say yes. Don't embarrass them by asking for something which, from their perspective, they barely have enough of. You may need to do more homework to find out.

9. *What is the person's self-interest in saying yes?*

How good would they feel saying yes? How sorry will they feel saying no? Is there enough positive self-interest? Ultimately, their emotional connection to your mission is what will sustain them as a lifelong donor.

10. *What concerns might this person have about saying yes to your request?*
Again, put yourself in the donor's shoes. Add in your worst
fears. Things like: the donor is still offended that we thanked him
too late for his last gift, the donor doesn't like the direction our
new program has taken, the donor's true allegiance was to our
former director—he doesn't like our new director as well. These
will be important for you to know so you can address them in the
cultivation process and not wait to address them in the Ask.

11. *What might strengthen this Ask?*
What could you add to the Ask that would make it nearly impossible for the person to say no: a different asker; an additional
asker; a memorial gift; a Leadership Gift; a Challenge or Matching
Gift; more years to spread out the payment; a particular type of
recognition?

12. *How would this person most like to be recognized?*
Donors will never bring up recognition. You must weave it into
the Ask. Let them know how "all donors at this level" will be
recognized—special receptions with the scholarship recipients,
meetings with important speakers, dinners at elegant homes, and
so on. Try to give them two or three options for recognition.

13. *How can this person invite others to participate?*
Once they have said yes, their natural tendency will be to want to
share their enthusiasm for this organization with others—it's good
to mention some of those opportunities during the Ask.

14. *What would be possible for your organization if the person says yes?*
Spend some time thinking through your response to this question,
not only what it would mean for your programs and services, but
what it could mean for the donor: perhaps she would like to be
asked to join your board. Think about the donor's Treasure Map.
Who else might they naturally want to involve or let you invite
to a Point of Entry?

15. *What other questions are still unanswered?*
If you have answered all of the above questions thoroughly, you
have probably uncovered some new ones. Remember, the more
armed you feel going into the Ask, the better.

If you are now able to answer each question in the list confidently, your donor is ready to be asked.

PREPARING THE ASKER

You've done the work. You've mapped out the football fields. Now, imagine that you've actually completed all the steps with at least one donor. Over the past three months to a year, you've come to know this person well. This donor loves your work, knows your needs, and has an emotional connection to your mission. Your consideration of the Pre-Ask Questions has shown you that you are truly at the end of the football field. The donor has given you all the "ready to be asked" signs.

Lest the pre-Ask "jitters" enter your thinking, as you prepare to make each Ask, remember the passion you have for the mission of your organization. Now, imagine that mission—fulfilled. Also, think about the donor's passion. Recall each donor's unique connection to your work. What has most piqued their interest about your group?

The process of asking is fun and natural. The biggest challenge is to remember that *it needs to be a dialog* between two people who already know each other.

You should practice asking each donor—twice—before you make the real Ask. It's fine to practice with the other people in your organization who may know these donors or the situation. You can even practice with a "stranger." Be sure to have the person or people who will be doing the asking be the ones to practice that part.

Brief the person you will be "asking" by answering these questions:
- What is this donor's past giving history with your organization?
- What are two or three concerns this donor might have about giving to you?
- Where will the Ask take place?
- What are your biggest fears in asking this person?

Here are some tips to help the asker with the Ask role play. Notice that the first part is a list of things to be sure to include in each

Ask. These are very useful to write down and practice in advance. The second part lists some suggested phrases to use during the Ask.

Asking One-on-One

Each Ask should:
- Include two appreciation statements.
- Include two references to the program or Emotional Hook for this donor.
- Include one reference to the larger mission of your organization.
- Address the donor's specific concerns.
- Tell how you would like to recognize this donor/gift.
- Be structured as a dialog—ask questions like:
  - What do you think of our plan to _____?
  - How does this all sound to you?

Possible phrases to use:
- You have been such a friend to our organization.
- We have something particular in mind that we wanted to talk to you about today.
- We wanted to come to you first, since you're already part of our family.
- We'd like to ask you to make a gift of $_____.
- Can we count on your support for this?
- We'd love to have you there (at the Ask Event) with us so you can see the difference your support will make.

We spend a lot of time on this asking role play in our workshops, and the thing we hear over and over again is how valuable the practice is for people. Even though the real Ask will be different when you do it, practicing helps you work through and anticipate many of the donor's concerns and discover in advance the donors who you really may not be ready to ask yet.

It bears repeating that if you are hesitating to ask, trust your instincts. If you have even the slightest sense that asking this person for money would be awkward or premature, then hold off asking until you have had another cultivation contact. The last thing you want is to have this donor be upset with you, after all the time you have taken to get to know one another.

Before I go to ask someone for money, I always put myself in their shoes. How would I like to be approached by two people, knowing full well what they want from me? Recall that this is an organization I love and will feel excited to support. I have been well cultivated. In fact, I feel that I have guided myself very naturally through the process. I am wondering why no one has asked me to give until now. I have given many readiness signs to this group, hosted an event in my home, and invited friends to Point of Entry Events. This is one of the two or three places I want to give my money. I love these people and support what they are up to.

In other words, as you practice asking in a role play situation prior to the real Ask, do not default to thinking you are asking a complete stranger. Likewise, if you are playing the role of donor, do not pretend you hardly know this group and that they are bothering you. Neither is true. This is a relationship. You know one another by now. You are all the way down the football field. The donor knows in advance that at this meeting they will be asked for money. In fact, they are looking forward to saying yes.

Let me digress here with some examples of major gift Asks. We have heard wonderful stories from several of our alumni groups about Ask meetings they had scheduled with potential major donors of $500,000 and above. One group had a lunchtime Ask for $1 million scheduled with the executive director, the board chair (who was also a major donor), and the donor, but on the day of the appointment, the donor had to cancel. Rather than postponing the meeting, the donor called that morning to apologize, insisting on knowing what the Ask would be for. Despite the executive director's attempts to hem and haw and reschedule the lunch so the Ask could take place in person, the donor persisted and the nervous executive director finally blurted out, "We were planning to ask you to give $1 million towards the capital campaign for our new building." The donor replied, "I'd be delighted to do that—just send me all the paperwork."

The moral of that story is to never underestimate the power of the highly personal donor cultivation work you will be doing. This same executive director, who has now raised over $10 million for this campaign, calls me often with amazing success stories and to ask me, "How can we get our pipeline filled even faster with these wonderful donors who truly understand and appreciate our work?"

But let's suppose you aren't getting millions of dollars over the phone. Let's assume you'll need to go out and meet with people to ask. What else does it take to be successful when you ask?

BE AUTHENTIC

Once you have thoroughly done your preparation, you need to put it all aside. At this point, asking should be nothing more than nudging the inevitable. You are asking people who already know and love your organization. You already know they have what you are asking for. You already know they are emotionally connected to you.

I recommend you go into the Ask with an entirely different agenda: in those few minutes, see how related and connected you can become with the donor. It is all about listening for every cue and being much more focused on what they are saying right now than on what you should say next.

The key to a successful Ask is you being a real human being—not a robot with a script, but a regular person who truly cares about this organization and this donor. The more authentic you can be, the better.

Asking someone for money is an intimate occasion. It can be serious, playful, short and to the point, or long and drawn-out. No two Asks are ever the same, because no two people are the same. I recommend you approach it more like your first dance with your new, lifelong dance partner. You may step on each others' toes, grumble and laugh a bit, but eventually you will get it right. As with dancing, one person is the leader. In asking for money, it should go without saying that the donor is the leader.

Even after doing all your cultivation, some donors may say no to part or all of what you ask for. Your job if they do say no is to thank them for being a friend of your organization and to ask if there are any other ways they would like to be involved. Then your job is to figure out how to ask them again in exactly the way they want to be asked, for exactly the thing they do want to say yes to. And then you ask them again, or have the perfect person ask them, so they say yes and feel great about it.

If they say yes and don't feel great about it, it's not a "win." You don't want to leave them with that icky feeling—that sense of having been manipulated into giving more than they were comfortable giving. You don't need their contribution that badly. You want each donor to feel as though they have sprinkled fairy dust on the most worthy organization in the world. You want each donor to feel so good about giving to you that they have no need for others to even know they did it. You want them to feel as if supporting your organization is a source of personal pleasure for them.

You have to let them know how excited you are to receive their gifts. You cannot be just a little bit appreciative. Let them know right away that their gifts are a big deal to you. Then you will have made a real friend. You have allowed them to truly contribute and feel the way you feel when you know you have made a real contribution.

Cultivating lifelong donors and connecting them to your work is the real nugget of the model. Once established and nurtured, that personal connection becomes the driver of the relationship.

Rather than giving out of guilt or obligation to a friend who is on your board, these donors have chosen to become—and remain—involved with you, for their own reasons. Multiply that by hundreds, even thousands of donors, and you can begin to see over the horizon to long-term sustainability for your organization.

CHAPTER 12

GROWING YOUR ASK EVENT RESULTS

With all this special one-on-one attention given to donors, you might wonder if it is even necessary to continue having Ask Events every year. The answer is an emphatic "yes!" The Ask Event serves several critical purposes in growing the model.

First, it focuses your efforts every year. Without an Ask Event, Point of Entry Events would languish. There would no longer be a sense of urgency to have more and more people come to Point of Entry Events.

Conversely, the Ask Event is a pre-Point of Entry of sorts. It whets people's appetites for more. It gives your Table Captains a purpose for inviting their friends to Point of Entry Events all year long—even after the Ask Event. And the Ask Event brings in people who wouldn't normally come to a Point of Entry.

Here are some additional reasons to keep having Ask Events:

- To keep you on track with the model.
- To seduce you into the world of major gifts.
- To give small to mid-sized donors an opportunity to start giving to you.
- To focus your implementation of the model and drive the timeline for each part of the process.
- To add urgency to having Point of Entry Events and doing follow up.
- To get focused on a Challenge or Leadership Gift.
- To keep board members and volunteers connected to the mission, even if they attend as VIPs.

- To showcase your work publicly in your community.
- To attract people who you wouldn't otherwise know or think to invite to a Point of Entry.
- To keep the rhythm of the cycle going round and round and spiraling up and up.
- To give Multiple-Year Donors an opportunity to make their annual pledge payment while they are inspired and reconnected.
- To allow Multiple-Year Donors to pay off or increase their pledge.
- To allow Multiple-Year Donors to see their community of friends who love and appreciate your organization.
- To remind donors of the difference their money makes.
- To generate new board members, team members, and volunteers.
- To remind everyone associated with the organization how proud they are to be associated with it.
- To allow you to honor any special donors or VIPs.
- To generate new Multiple-Year Donors each year (10%-15% of the guests).

CELEBRATE YOUR SUCCESS

Before we begin the process of designing your future Ask Events, take a moment to pat yourself on the back for the great job you did on your first Ask Event. Whatever your degree of success or adherence to the model, if your group actually held an Ask Event, you have no doubt learned a lot.

Perhaps the amount of money you raised met or exceeded our formula (total number of Ask Event guests divided by two and then multiplied by $1,000; for example, a 200-person event should raise at least $100,000 including the five-year pledges). Congratulations!

You can also see that the event brought your group a lot more than money. For one, the Ask Event helped you tell your organization's story to your community. For most of the groups we train and coach, over 60% of their Ask Event donors are brand-new donors.

As guests left the one-hour event, many told their Table Captains that they wanted to discuss a gift with their spouse or with someone at their company or charitable foundation. People mentioned other in-kind gifts, like office space or land for your new building or a new vehicle. They wanted you to come out to speak to their employee group or their civic club. Your organization was the talk of the town for a day or a week after the event.

Another benefit of having one Ask Event or more under your belt is that now you are hooked. Compared to the other labor-intensive special events your group has been doing, this event was far easier to do. There were no auction items to procure, no tickets to sell, no fancy food to order. In short, you didn't need to worry about entertaining people with a good party. You could rely on what your organization does best—your mission—to be the centerpiece of the event.

Your inside team was reconnected. Board members, even those who may have been skeptical about the process, were inspired and proud. To sit in a room of 100 to 200 people and have them be moved and inspired by the organization's work is a dream come true for a board member. Their community is discovering what they've known all along—that your group is doing effective, life-changing work every day. In the space of those sixty minutes, they could feel the stature of the organization rising in the eyes of the guests.

So hooray, hallelujah, jump up and down, pat yourself on the back—you did it!

ASK EVENT CHALLENGES IN YEAR TWO AND BEYOND

One thing we hear after the Ask Event, from every single group, regardless of how much money they raised in that hour, is that they now see all the things they could have done to make the event even better and they are determined to get to work right away while their success is fresh.

Meeting the Measures

Let's review what we're aiming for:

First, your Ask Event must meet or exceed our basic "formula" goal each year. Beyond that, five of our top ten measures on the Sustainable Funding Scorecard are met at the Ask Event. They are:

1. After year one, at least 40% of Ask Event attendees have attended a Point of Entry prior to the Ask Event (also known as the 40% "ripened fruit" rule).
2. At least 40% of Ask Event guests make a gift or pledge on the day of the event.
3. At least 5%–10% of Ask Event attendees give at the $1,000 (for five years) level.
4. At least 10%–15% of Ask Event attendees join the Multiple-Year Giving Society each year (at one of your three giving levels).
5. Announce a Challenge or Leadership Gift of increasing size at each Ask Event.

Whether your first Ask Event met the formula or not, it's possible to meet all of these measures the second time around and beyond—if you are implementing the full model as we have described. Let's look at each measure one by one.

Clearly, the most critical predictor of success is the **40% "ripened fruit" rule**. In the first year, we require only 20% of your Ask Event guests to have attended a prior Point of Entry. But from the second event and thereafter, we up that percentage to 40%. This is for several reasons. First, we have found that Ask Event guests who attended a prior Point of Entry are more than twice as likely to join your Multiple-Year Giving Society at your Ask Event. Second, our groups that tally up total giving at the Ask Event and then divide the money raised into two categories—people who have or have not attended a Point of Entry—find that more than 80% of the total money raised at their Ask Events comes from the prior Point of Entry guest group. The more "ripened fruit" at your event, the better the results will be. Groups that have 80%–90% of their guests in this category raise several times more money than those with only 40%.

After the first Ask Event, all of our groups recognize this correlation between Point of Entry guests and Ask Event results, and they suddenly become more interested in implementing the full model.

They recognize that for the same amount of work it takes to put on an Ask Event, they can multiply their bottom-line results by taking time to more fully cultivate their donors before the event.

As I said in Chapter 3 when we discussed the scorecard measures, **having at least 40%–50% of your Ask Event guests make a gift or pledge on the day of the event** should not be difficult after the first Ask Event. Just be careful that your percentages don't get much higher than 50%–60% or you should be suspicious of strong-arming. Also, if you meet the 40%–50% of guests giving measure, be sure that those aren't all small donors. In addition to meeting this measure, you must be sure to meet the next two as well.

Each year, **at least 5%–10% of your Ask Event attendees make new pledges to give at the $1,000 a year (for five years) level**. This is what keeps the pipeline filled for future Leadership Gifts, Challenge Gifts, and major gifts. And it will only happen if you have been doing the Point of Entry work.

Next, 10%–15% of your Ask Event attendees join the Multiple-Year Giving Society each year (at any one of your three giving levels). In other words, we want to be seeing more large donors than just the 5%–10% at the lowest level. We look for 10% of your Multiple-Year Giving Society paying off their pledges in full the second year and 20% of the Multiple-Year Giving Society Donors increasing or extending their gift each year.

Finally, **announce a Leadership or Challenge Gift of increasing size each year** at your Ask Event. The impact of announcing this gift at the event is huge. People notice—they notice that others are supporting your group in a big way. They notice that you have stepped up your focus and level of sophistication about securing larger gifts. This may help to subtly reposition your organization in their minds to being the type of group they might now consider for a larger gift. Also, if you can have the donor or one of the donors (if it is a pooled gift) speak at the event—ideally right before the Pitch—to say why they chose to give this gift, it will be compelling and might just inspire a few others in the audience to make bigger gifts right then.

Of course, as we have said, if it is structured as a Challenge Gift, it must be announced right before the Pitch, clearly explaining the "rules" of the challenge (such as a two-to-one match for every new member of the Multiple-Year Giving Society) and the deadline after which the challenge expires.

One other thing to consider, under the category of Leadership Gifts, is having a sponsor. Having the event sponsored by a corporation or foundation that already knows you and supports your work also adds credibility and lets every dollar people give go right to the bottom line. You can determine the dollar amount of the sponsorship. At a minimum, it should cover the costs of putting on the event.

As your event grows in size and stature each year, you may be able to raise the price of the sponsorship and offer more visibility for the corporation than they would have received for sponsoring your golf tournament or other smaller special event. One organization we work with received a $250,000 sponsor for their large Ask Event. Although their costs to put on their event were under $20,000, the sponsor happily made the gift knowing that it would go to the operating needs of the group.

Ideally, you will have only one significant sponsor, headed by a person or group of people who really understands and appreciates your work. Perhaps they have been involved as volunteers or beneficiaries of your work. In addition to making a large sponsorship gift, they may participate in the Ask Event program, perhaps as a Testimonial Speaker or the Pitch Person.

While these formulas may seem steep, if you are implementing the model for the purpose it is designed—with a goal of building long-term sustainable funding—these will be welcome benchmarks to tell you that you are on the right track.

Size of Event

When people hear that they will be doing Ask Events forever, they fear the event will need to be larger each year and that they will eventually run out of people to invite. In fact, we do not recommend growing the size of your Ask Event after the third year.

You want your event to get to the size that works best for you and let it plateau there. If you must have a larger event, consider having two events per year—one larger and one smaller event in a private club or more intimate setting. The smaller event can be the source of larger Challenge or Leadership Gifts to be announced at the larger event.

Overconfidence / Community Perception

The second-year Ask Event is no time to put up your feet and presume you know what you are doing. Many groups find their results plummet the second year due to overconfidence, "laziness," or "creativity" with the model.

On the contrary, this second event is critical. While the first event may have brought in a lot of money, there will still be skeptics who know that last year you had plenty of ripened fruit to pick: you never did the requisite number of Point of Entry Events, your Point of Entry Events were lackluster, you defaulted to pressuring staff and board members to be Table Captains, etc.

This is the year people will be watching to see if you can pull it off again. If your first event was extremely successful, the naysayers will be waiting in the wings, ready to remind you that the gala or golf tournament was a tried and true winner. And they will be right. *Putting on the Ask Event is not the same thing as implementing the model.*

Conversely, if you have followed the model, done the proper follow up after the first Ask Event, and met face-to-face with each of your Multiple-Year Donors once or twice during the ensuing year, you will be well-positioned to grow the model.

Also, if you did well the first year, people may wonder why you still need money. Each subsequent event needs to thank the loyal donors for their generous gifts, tell them what their gifts have allowed you to do, and clearly convey the next level of needs.

Of course, there are some ways in which the second year is easier than the first. No doubt, you have won over some of the skeptics. Perhaps they are willing to jump in now as Table Captains. You may have uncovered one or more contenders to be sponsors or Challenge Gift donors for next year's event.

With your second time around, you often have more time to get an early start on all the preparation work. You now know the ropes; you have conquered the fear of the unknown. You can focus on refining and improving upon your first event—not starting from scratch. How can you ensure the excitement and energy of a full room, bustling with full tables, and an even bigger bottom line the next time?

Encouraging Repeat Guests

Most groups are surprised to find that 30%–50% of their second-year Ask Event guests also attended the first year's event. It is like going back to a favorite movie or a favorite restaurant—you don't get tired of it. In fact, if anything, you are excited to invite friends to have that same wonderful experience you had.

Repeat guests include Table Captains, donors, staff, volunteers, and board members. They return for the same reason as everyone else: because they love the organization and the event reconnects them. It is a great place to see the people associated with the organization. For many donors, this is their one time in the year when they can pay their annual pledge in person. A surprising percentage of donors will choose to pay off the remaining four years of their pledge and some will choose to increase or extend their pledge.

Remember: this model is about building lifelong donors. For many of your first-time Multiple-Year Donors, their gift will be the first of many gifts of increasing size. This is part of the new reality of committed donors to your organization—you will need to get used to it!

Changing the Program

The number one concern that people have the second time around is, ironically, not with developing a stronger audience who will be more prepared to give, but with the program for the event.

A New Theme Each Year

We generally recommend that your event have a theme each year and that you tie that theme to your needs. At the school where we designed the model, the Ask Event is still called the Sponsor-a-Student Breakfast, but the theme changes each year. One year we used a "back to school" theme. Other years we focused on the dreams of our students, on alumni stories, on supportive family members, and on the teachers.

This way, though the generic program elements remain the same—Visionary Leader Talk, video, Testimonial Speaker, etc.—the program content is very different each year.

For example, in the year that our theme was "supportive families," the Visionary Leader Talk was about the essential role of the families in ensuring each child's success at the school. The Testimonial Speaker was a grandmother who spoke about the impact of the school on her grandson. The video included three stories of traditional and non-traditional families whose children were attending the school.

The Visionary Leader Talk is a good opportunity to link your theme to your organization's mission. Phrases like, "our dream is to not have to turn away any family with a child in need," can tie your vision to the theme. Rely on your mission statement for the overarching vision; people never tire of that.

So, keep the name and the program elements of your Ask Event the same each year, but let each year's theme determine the focus of the program elements.

Modifying the Pitch

Use your second Ask Event as an opportunity to honor the founding members of the Multiple-Year Giving Society who made their first pledge the year before. It is fine to ask them to stand up to be recognized at the event. Many groups choose to print their names on the back of the programs. That way, when it comes time for the Pitch, others in the audience will see that this is an ongoing society they might want to support. Also, the second-year Pitch can allude to some of the things the first year's funding made possible—raising teachers' salaries or offering tuition reductions.

We usually recommend modifying the script to say: "We invite you to join with our founding members as we grow our giving society."

Then, as your Pitch Person goes through the giving levels, be sure to call attention to the special section (which can be on the back of the pledge form) for prior donors to pay off and/or increase their pledge. At this point, the Pitch Person can say something like this: "Some of you here today also attended this event last year and pledged your support. We thank you sincerely. We have a special section on the back of the pledge sheet just for you."

The back of the pledge sheet should contain the following options for your prior donors:

I would like to pay my pledge in the following way:

❑ Add _____ more years to my previous multiple-year pledge.

❑ Increase my financial commitment by $_____ for _____ years.

❑ Pay off my outstanding pledge in full and increase to $_____ for _____ years.

❑ My annual pledge payment is enclosed.

❑ Please contact me. I have other thoughts to share.

Units of Service

If you followed the model in designing your levels the first year, your levels should stay the same for at least ten years. If you deviated from the model and started with lower amounts or less than five-year pledges, you will find yourself in an awkward dilemma. While you will see the value of changing your levels, it can be complicated to explain the change to first-year donors who thought they were giving in precisely the way you wanted them to. In this case, it is worth readjusting your levels at year two, to better position your organization for the future.

Don't Mess with the Recipe

One major pitfall we find with subsequent Ask Events is the temptation to deviate from the formula—to "get creative." Changing the time of year, changing the dollar levels of your Units of Service, adding in other items to the pledge card (like the mention of a capital campaign or endowment), or adding a more traditional outside speaker to the program, will each lead you astray.

Two of the other biggest mistakes groups often make in subsequent Ask Events are not related to the program at all, but rather have to do with that key leverage point: the Table Captains. First, there is the temptation to rely more and more on board members to be your core group of Table Captains. The fastest way for an event to stagnate and ultimately fail over time is to have this be just another version of strong-arming the board to invite their same group of friends to fill a table. Second, there is the corollary to that: the need for new Table Captains each year. This requires diligent monthly Point of Entry Events where at least 25% of the guests refer others to subsequent Point of Entry Events.

If, even for one year, you slack off on the model, you will see the results in the bottom line of your Ask Event. The formula is so clearly spelled out and easy to follow—you should not need to make these mistakes. Rather, you should experience increasingly successful Ask Events each year as the model grows your base of mission-centered lifelong individual donors.

FOLLOW THE ENTIRE MODEL

This is often the point where groups realize that the process of putting on the Ask Event, including the results, has begun to change the way the entire organization does its fundraising. Moreover, many groups tell us that at this point, they can also see how the model affects their marketing, their volunteer and board recruitment, and even the way the program staff feel about their jobs.

This is the perfect time to solidify everyone's buy-in to the over-all Benevon system and renew their commitment to employ a more mission-focused fundraising process going forward. This is the time to ask your board for a five-year commitment to following the model. If you are serious about developing a self-sustaining funding base, now is the time to shore up your support and invest in growing your program. This is the point at which many organizations reassemble their implementation team for the next year, adding one or more staff members to focus solely on implementing the model.

These groups recognize that the personalized cultivation process will pay off in funds raised and other support. They see that the Multiple-Year Giving Society could expand each year, leading to more significant major donors. They realize this has all been worth the risk and they are ready to invest some of their hard-earned resources into growing the program.

Groups often ask us if people will tire of the event. They wonder why prior donors would want to come back to another Ask Event the next year. Ultimately, they are concerned that there is a limit to such a good thing.

However, like your organization's mission, the Benevon Model is built to last. Many groups have been following the model for many years. The school where the model was developed recently held its eleventh annual Sponsor-a-Student Breakfast, once again with outstanding results.

There are many ways to spruce up your event each year, while still being true to the model and to your mission. The most important factor for increasing your Ask Event results year after year is having passionate Table Captains.

CHAPTER 13

TABLE CAPTAIN RECRUITMENT

While there are many strategies for increasing the bottom line at your Ask Event, the single most crucial factor for increasing your results year after year and keeping your audience fresh and enthusiastic is the passion of your Table Captains.

Therefore, most groups learn from experience with their first Ask Event that the earlier they focus on recruiting and tending Table Captains who are passionate, the stronger the event will be.

Ultimately, since you can determine the size of the event you want to have a full year in advance, you can plan and implement each step of the Table Captain recruitment timeline sanely over the course of the year.

The first step is to determine the number of Table Captains you will need, which is a function of the size you want your Ask Event to be. We encourage most groups to plateau the size of their Ask Event by the third or fourth year, relying on more "ripened fruit" and Leadership/Challenge Gifts to continually increase their bottom line, without having to add more people. The second and third year's Ask Events are the right time to scale your event to the ideal size and then plan on keeping it at about that size.

This is a good point to mention the possibility of reducing the size of your Ask Event. Some groups are overwhelmed the first year and wonder how to project realistically for future years. Choose a size that is manageable for your group, considering the number of Table Captains to be recruited and tended. Remember that you still need to go through all the steps to put on the event, regardless of the number of people attending, so choose a number that makes all of your effort worthwhile.

INCREASING TABLE CAPTAIN PASSION

Knowing that the number one criterion for a great Table Captain is passion for your organization's mission, there is no need to default to people who are easy to recruit out of their obligation to or familiarity with the organization—people whose passion may have waned a bit over time.

After all, which of these phone calls would you like your Table Captains to make when they invite their guests?

- *Would you come sit at my table at a fundraising event for the autism nonprofit group here in town? I told them I'd put a table together, and it would help me a lot if you'd come. You don't even have to give money.*

- *Remember the autism group I mentioned the last time we talked? They are amazing! I had no idea they were doing so much to help families and people with autism. I offered to be a Table Captain at their fundraising event because I was so impressed with their work in our community. I'd love for you to join me at my table this year. There is truly no obligation to give. We want people to come to learn about their work, as much as anything.*

As you look to your lists of passionate volunteers, board members, and donors, tell the truth about their current level of passion for your mission. Perhaps there is a volunteer with a family member who was directly affected by the problems or issues your organization is seeking to eradicate. If she were to become a Table Captain, the people she would invite to attend the Ask Event would likely say yes and attend because they know how much your work means to her.

Ideally, this woman would have invited several of her friends to Point of Entry Events prior to the Ask Event. These friends would have seen the work of the organization firsthand and, in the Follow-Up Call from a staff member or volunteer, would have had an opportunity to choose to become more involved. Therefore, several of the people at this woman's table at the Ask Event would be familiar enough with the mission of the organization that their gifts would not be made strictly because of a sense of guilt and obligation to their friend the Table Captain, but because they actually believe in your work.

If you begin to use passion as your main criterion for selecting Table Captains, you will have happier Table Captains *and* better financial results.

Passion Retread

Now let's revisit those dear friends of the organization who served as Table Captains merely because you asked them. While they may have had two or three empty seats at their table, they did the job, like good soldiers. Perhaps their passion for the organization was not naturally transmitted to their guests, yet once they got to the event, the passion was rekindled.

An effective strategy for increasing Table Captain passion—and therefore Ask Event size and results—is to focus on a Passion Retread for these trusted insiders. If you have ever been a long-term board member or volunteer with an organization, you will know how your initial passion can wane, and being asked to fill a table at another event feels like a burden and an obligation, rather than a privilege.

A method for rekindling their passion is to do this simple Passion Retread exercise at your next board or committee meeting or retreat. When people introduce themselves at the beginning of the session, have them tell their story of how they got involved or what keeps them involved with the organization. While many may say they got involved before they really understood the work being done, their reasons for staying involved now will be very moving. Often they will have a personal story or incident that instantly reconnects them.

This is also an excellent team-building exercise for boards or committees. I remember doing this exercise at a board retreat where one of the most outspoken and critical members told his story briefly. The organization had saved his son's life, thanks to one of their special programs, for which this man remained a staunch advocate. Just hearing him tell his story gave everyone a deep sense of compassion for his commitment to the program. You can bet that this man made an excellent Table Captain with a full table of people who understood the value of the organization.

TABLE CAPTAIN KICK-OFF

Another way to keep people excited about the Ask Event is by having a Table Captain kick-off meeting about ten weeks prior to your Ask Event. Even if you don't get 100% attendance, this event helps build momentum and rally the troops. It also gives you a reason to be in touch with those Table Captains who may need a little support in getting started even thinking about the process. Whenever I talk about Table Captains, I feel a need to state the obvious: any Table Captain who is unable to attend the Table Captain kick-off must receive a full briefing—either in person or over the telephone—to go over every item in the Table Captain packet that has been sent to them.

Here is the agenda for the Table Captain kick-off. The best overall reference on Table Captains as well as all the timelines, templates, and scripts you will need to put on a powerful Ask Event every year is *The Ask Event Handbook.*

TABLE CAPTAIN KICK-OFF AGENDA
FREE ONE-HOUR ASK EVENT

Welcome	Executive Director	Thank people for attending and explain the importance of the Ask Event and their essential role in its success.	3 min.
Introductions	Executive Director	Introduce your team and your Team Leader who will be coordinating the event. Introduce any board members in attendance. Then take time for each person to introduce themselves and state how they are connected to the organization, including why they care about the organization.	10 min.
Overview of Benevon Model	Team Leader/ Development Director	Using handouts of the model or a flip chart, the Team Leader explains the four steps of the model and where the Ask Event fits into the larger process of cultivating lifelong relationships with mission-focused donors.	5 min.
Ask Event Program Overview	Team Leader/ Development Director	The person responsible for the event walks everyone through the program for the event, step by step. Take questions as you go through this.	10 min.

continued on next page

continued from previous page

TABLE CAPTAIN KICK-OFF AGENDA
FREE ONE-HOUR ASK EVENT

Treasure Map for the Organization	Team Leader/ Development Director	Draw out a quick Treasure Map on a flip chart or overhead projector, or show them the Treasure Map your team has already prepared. Highlight the many groups that already know about your work and might want to attend the event, including the group called "Point of Entry Guests," many of whom have now been cultivated and are ready to be asked to contribute financially.	5 min.
Personal Treasure Map for Each Table Captain	Team Leader/ Development Director	Have each Table Captain make a personal Treasure Map of the people they come into contact with on a regular basis, in their work or personal lives. Be sure to cover what resources these people have in abundance and what might be their self-interest in learning more about the organization. End by having each Table Captain make a list of at least thirty people from their personal Treasure Map they could invite to sit at their table at the Ask Event. People often become very excited at this point. They bring out their address books and personal planners. Be prepared for some people to tell you that they would like to host more than one table—this should be a natural outcome of this part of the kick-off agenda.	10 min.
Table Captain Packet Review	Team Leader/ Development Director	Hand out the Table Captain packets and walk people through the contents. Be sure to include how you will stay in contact with the Table Captains from now until the day of the event, either by phone, fax, or e-mail. Let them know you will be contacting them often.	5 min.
Questions	Team Leader/ Executive Director	Give people plenty of time to ask questions. You want them to leave the kick-off reconnected to their passion for the organization and excited and confident about the Ask Event and their role in it.	10 min.
Thank You and Close	Executive Director	Be sure to take the time to tell your Table Captains how much you appreciate them. Tell them how you will be in touch with them from now until the day of the event.	1 min.
		Total time:	56 min.

YEAR-ROUND RECRUITMENT

All year long, be on the lookout for the people who are most excited and dedicated to your work. In fact, the best time to start your next year's Table Captain recruitment is in the week following your Ask Event as you are making your Follow-Up Calls.

Part of the standard Ask Event follow-up procedure is to call each Table Captain the day after the event to thank them and ask what their guests said as they walked away from the event. Did they mention that they wanted to go home and talk to someone about giving to the organization? Are they affiliated with a corporation or foundation that they wanted to talk with before making a gift?

Odds are, your Table Captains will be excited! They will tell you who said what, how much they loved the event, and perhaps give you feedback on parts they feel could be improved. Special note: Don't get defensive when they do this; instead, listen closely to their feedback and thank them for it. Assume that you might have had that same feedback had you been a guest at your event. If appropriate, consider how you can incorporate their advice for your next Ask Event.

Your Table Captains will likely also tell you about people they wished had attended, like, "I was so sorry Angela couldn't be there. She would have loved it!" As you are listening to their feedback, it will be very natural to tell them the date of next year's event and ask them if they would agree to be a Table Captain again.

We have many groups that secure 50%–60% of their Table Captains within two weeks of the preceeding Ask Event. Of course, it helps if you have locked in the date of your next Ask Event before you make your Follow-Up Calls.

Here is a scenario and timeline for Table Captain Recruitment.

TABLE CAPTAIN RECRUITMENT PLAN

1. Today's date: _____

2. Next Ask Event date: _____

3. Financial goal: $300,000

4. Number of guests: 400

5. Starting number of Table Captains needed: 55

6. Person accountable _____ for having _55_ Table Captains by _____ (date). (Table Captain recruitment must be complete by six weeks before the Ask Event.)

	9 Months Prior	6 Months Prior	3 Months Prior	10 Weeks Prior	6 Weeks Prior	Ask Event Date
Date						
# of Table Captains	10	25	40	Table Captain Kick-off	55	47

Notice that we are aiming to have 400 people at the next event, which would be double the number we had at the first event. Recall that you will not need to increase the size of the event forever. As I said earlier, by your third Ask Event, you should have reached the size you will stay at long-term. (For example, many groups start with a first Ask Event of 100 people, a second event of 200 people, and a third event of 300 people, which is where they plateau.)

Using our formulas of 15% attrition of Table Captains and then 15% attrition of the guests of the remaining Table Captains, if you are aiming to have 400 people at the event, you would need to start the process with fifty-five potential Table Captains.

DETERMINING THE NUMBER OF TABLE CAPTAINS YOU NEED

Number of Ask Event Guests in Attendance	Number of Table Captains You Need to Start With
100	14
150	21
200	28
250	35
300	43
400	55
500	68
700	97
1000	138

We say that you need to have the full number of Table Captains confirmed by six weeks before the event. Working backwards from that six-weeks-out date, plot out the number of Table Captains you will need every three months prior to that.

Notice that this timeline starts immediately after the prior Ask Event, but that will be no problem for you because you will have many Table Captains already committed based on the Follow-Up Calls from your first event.

Still, fifty-five Table Captains is a big number. Let's look at where else these new Table Captains might naturally come from. First, as we said, let's assume that your first event had 200 guests and met our scorecard formulas as far as giving. Of the twenty Table Captains you had the first year, ten agree to do it again. Plus, let's say fourteen other guests from your new Multiple-Year Donors agree to be Table Captains next year.

You now have twenty-four Table Captains—you are nearly halfway to your year-two target of fifty-five Table Captains. Where will you find the remaining thirty-one Table Captains?

TREASURE MAP: FOUR TARGET GROUPS

Look back to your Treasure Map and to the list you made in Chapter 7 of the four Treasure Map groups you will focus on inviting to Point of Entry Events this year, the twenty people from each group you could invite to Point of Entry Events, and the number of potential Table Captains you have targeted from each of those four target groups.

TABLE CAPTAIN STRATEGY

1. Today's date: _____
2. Month/date of Ask Event: _____
3. Targeted number of guests at Ask Event: _____
4. Number of Table Captains you must start with: _____
5. Minimum number of guests who must attend Point of Entry (at least 40% of #3 above): _____
6. How many Table Captains will come from each group on your Treasure Map? _____

Treasure Map Group	Names of Potential Point of Entry Guests				Targeted Number of Potential Table Captains
			Total Table Captains:		

Once your team commits to finding a total of fifty-five Table Captains, your minds will start to work on it. Everyone you invite to a Point of Entry Event will become someone you consider as a potential Table Captain. You will naturally ask yourself: Is this someone with real passion for our work? Is this someone who would commit to fill a table of ten people and follow through with that commitment?

Also, doing a personal Treasure Map exercise each year with your board members (see Chapter 17) is another source of Point of Entry guests and, ultimately, Table Captains.

SECONDARY INVITATION STRATEGY

One last tool you have available to you to meet your targeted number of Table Captains for next year's event is what we refer to as the Secondary Invitation Strategy for making sure everyone gets invited to the Ask Event. Going forward, it is essential because there is no guarantee that people who came to your prior Ask Events will automatically be invited by a Table Captain the next year, and you certainly wouldn't want to offend them by not inviting them.

We refer to it as the Secondary Invitation Strategy because the primary strategy is what we have already been discussing: having your Table Captains invite their friends and associates personally, usually by telephone or e-mail, with many of their friends attending Point of Entry Events before the Ask Event.

This secondary strategy allows your organization to serve as one big "Table Captain" to invite everyone else who has attended a prior Point of Entry or Ask Event who will not necessarily be included on the guest list of a Table Captain.

Here are the steps to follow to implement the Secondary Invitation Strategy:

1. Make a list of these key people: all prior Point of Entry guests, prior donors, former board members, volunteers, corporate sponsors, and anyone else in the community who has asked to learn more.

2. Have your key staff/board members review this list to determine the best person to call each of these guests—someone with whom they have a personal relationship.

3. Have the identified person invite the people on their list, following the same process as the Table Captain process: telephone or in-person invitation, "Save-the-Date" card mailed, and a reminder call made two or three days before the event.

4. Decide where to seat these special guests:
   a. Included at staff and board tables (it's fine for them to fill more than one table).
   b. At a special VIP table.
   c. Matched up with someone they know.
   d. At tables where a Table Captain is having difficulty filling his/her table (be sure to tell the appropriate Table Captain in advance that this guest will be joining them).

AN ABUNDANCE OF RESOURCES

As we conclude this discussion of Table Captain recruitment, I hope you can see the abundance of passionate people you have surrounding your organization, people to invite to Point of Entry Events, to invite to be Table Captains, to come to your Ask Events, and ultimately to become lifelong supporters.

There really is no need to resort to thinking that you don't have enough potential Table Captains or to pressure your board or staff to become Table Captains to help you out because you are desperate. Everyone who participates in the implementation of the model needs to do so willingly and happily, because they believe in your work and truly want to be part of your success.

Once the model takes off in an organization, it will pick up steam and generate an abundance of new passionate people.

CHAPTER 14

AFTER THE ASK—
DEEPENING THE RELATIONSHIP

If you are following the model closely, you can already sense that asking for money—whether one-on-one or at an Ask Event—is the culmination of a process, not a way to start a relationship. We say that the Ask shouldn't be a big scary event with a stranger—it should be one more natural contact along the Cultivation Superhighway.

Likewise, we don't abandon our donors after they have given generously. That is precisely the time to stay connected. By continuing to tend and nurture them along the Cultivation Superhighway, these same major donors will keep giving, often in substantially increasing amounts. This is how the cycle begins to spiral upwards.

Let's look at what cultivation looks like after someone becomes a member of your Multiple-Year Giving Society.

We have three measures on our Sustainable Funding Scorecard that address this point in the cycle. If you are aiming to grow the model towards sustainable funding, you must have:

1. At least two in-person or phone cultivation contacts with each Multiple-Year Donor each year.
2. An annual Master Cultivation Calendar in place and being followed (even for donors who don't attend Free Feel-Good Cultivation Events).
3. Two or more Free Feel-Good Cultivation Events per year with 50% of your Multiple-Year Donors attending at least one each year.

Those are some steep measures to meet, especially as the model grows and you have more and more major donors.

The first step is having a Master Cultivation Calendar in place and being followed for all donors. We discussed an outline for that plan in Chapter 8, in terms of cultivation leading up to a big Ask.

Once a donor has been on your Next Ten Asks list, cultivated through the steps of the football field, and ultimately makes a gift, that donor remains on your cultivation calendar in whichever new donor category they belong. For example, a donor who was on your Next Ten Ask list who just made a Leadership Gift of $25,000 a year for the next five years, would move up to the Multiple-Year Donor section under the highest multiple-year level. Eventually you will need to add new categories to that chart for donors who give more than your highest giving society level such as "more than $25,000 for five years." Of course, there is also the category called One-Time Donors, for those major donors who do not make a multiple-year pledge. Those are still major donors! You need a full cultivation plan mapped out for each of them as well.

Some of the cultivation activities will be group activities, like Free Feel-Good Cultivation Events, be it a graduation ceremony, a special awards ceremony, or a home dedication for a Habitat new homeowner. Other events will be individual cultivation activities, which also need to be systematically mapped out and put on someone's individual work calendar on a particular date to ensure that they happen.

This is how the major universities conduct such masterful major gifts programs. It's not that their mission is necessarily any more compelling than any other group's mission, but rather, over the years, they have continued to cultivate—slowly tend and nurture, step by step, systematically—their relationship with each potential donor.

Take the example of a college student. From the minute a student is accepted to a university, they are on the radar of the "Advancement Office." Having two children currently in college, this example is a fresh one for me. Our entire family has been carefully watched by these universities from the moment the acceptance letters arrived. As parents, we are invited to parent weekends, sporting events, and (very soon!) graduation ceremonies. But our children are being tended and nurtured as well. They are asked to be part of a "class gift" to their respective schools, and then asked to become annual donors, even at a small level, just to get the "habit" developed. Through strategically timed magazines, newsletters, and live events such as reunions, "football weekends," etc., they stay connected—emotionally—to their friends and teachers, but even more so to their memories. The Emotional Hook for a great university is nostalgia and a sense of gratitude—wanting to give back, which can take a few years to develop after graduation.

Slowly but surely, over the years, those annual gifts become larger, alumni reunions are held at various major cities around the country, deans make personal calls to key alumni, phone-a-thons from current students tug at the heartstrings, and before we know it, we are being asked for more significant gifts, and—willingly—giving them. Every few years, the university has such a large "batch" of donors who have been well-cultivated and are ready to make significant contributions, as well as plenty of new needs for buildings, labs, stadiums, libraries, and scholarships, that they decide it is time to lump all of this big giving into a campaign.

Unlike many smaller nonprofits that try to ramp up retroactively in response to a sudden capital need (e.g., a new building), for these universities, there is relatively little risk in the process. That's because they know their donors, they have been related to them since they were eighteen years old, and the donors have that deep emotional connection and sense of gratitude. At that point in the cycle, those donors are ready to give. There is nothing forced or unnatural about it.

This is precisely what we hear from the groups in our upper-level programs. Even with only three to five years of implementing the model, they are beginning to see remarkable results. While their donors are generally not "alumni" of their programs (e.g., a homeless shelter—not a university), it is possible, using the model, for any nonprofit to connect with potential donors at an emotional level and then systematically cultivate and nurture them.

The Multiple-Year Giving Society is the threshold for major gifts. It separates those who are serious about you from those who are just checking you out. Looking back to the university example, they know that not all alumni become major donors. Those universities are grateful for every single donor, even those who give any amount to their "annual funds" one year at a time.

Using our model, those Multiple-Year Giving Society Donors have self-selected to become your new best friends. Their five-year commitment is an enormous signal that they care about your mission. While for many of these donors, $1,000 a year is hardly a huge gift, it is their way of giving you permission to come back and keep tending and nurturing that relationship going forward. And we see how quickly that relationship can grow; 20% of these donors pay off that five-year pledge by the second year. Rather than running away from that commitment, they are anxious to get you their money even sooner, and 10% of those donors pay off that pledge and increase it by the second year!

Those statistics don't just happen magically. They happen because of the smart staff, board members, and volunteers who are following the model by focusing right away, after their Ask Events or one-on-one Asks, on personally cultivating that donor in precisely the way they now know that donor needs to be tended. Those cultivation steps may not be 100% predictable at the time that each Ask is completed. But they still must meet our scorecard measure of a minimum of twice a year personal contact with each Multiple-Year Donor.

The easiest way to accomplish this, once you have reached this point in implementing the model, is to put it all in the chart, offsetting group contacts (Free Feel-Good Cultivation Events) with individual contacts every quarter of the year. For example, in January, have a personal contact with all donors at the very highest level. The executive director (just like a college dean or president) could phone or have lunch with each of the major donors. Stratify the donors to make this doable. The super high level donors would have a one-on-one lunch meeting. The next tier down might be invited to a special small group private reception to hear from the top research scientist in that field, or to have a private dinner with the CEO and board president (or, better yet, with the entire board!) to thank them and share the next dreams and challenges of the organization. While this is in fact a group cultivation event, it will feel very personal and special to each donor.

Blocking out one hour a week in the calendar of a busy CEO to make these calls will pay big dividends. Ideally, the calls have been pre-scheduled by an assistant to ensure actually reaching the donor at the time the CEO is available. But I know of several CEOs who use this hour to call donors even at lower giving levels, just to say thank you, leaving voicemail messages. Another great use of that hour is to have the CEO personally sign thank-you letters. Although a letter does not allow for a meaningful dialog right in the moment, it makes an impression on the donor—and right there in the note the CEO can say "I'd like to give you a call next week," or "I am looking forward to talking with you (or seeing you) soon."

So plot out on your Master Cultivation Calendar these events, first by each category of donor (more than $25,000 for five years, etc.), and then look to see what would be the most appropriate type of contact for each individual donor. Remember that by then you will know them well enough to know their preferences and personalities. A lot of the mystery will be gone. It will be more like tending a relationship with a friend.

Set a goal of having at least two personal contacts with each donor per year. And remember, a telephone call counts as a contact.

CEO TIME

This last discussion might have prompted some concern about the amount of CEO time needed to effectively implement the model at the higher levels. I was recently asked by a board member at our 301 Workshop, "Just how much time should our CEO be spending on all of this?" My reply: "Somewhere between 20% and 80% of his time." I went on, fairly forcefully, asking, "What else does a CEO have to do that is more important—and for which he or she is uniquely qualified—than this?" Much to my delight, everyone on their team nodded in relief. People who ask that question already see the direct correlation between CEO time spent cultivating and bottom-line fundraising results. This is the point at which many CEOs admit that they really enjoy this type of cultivation. They have now been coached to speak powerfully about their missions, and they realize they are not "begging" for a handout, but rather they are asking people to get involved with a mission they already care about. In other words, they begin to see that they are helping donors do something that is meaningful to them. And who better than the CEO to explain to the donor what every dollar will be used for?

Even the more reluctant CEOs begin to see the value in setting aside time for donor cultivation and asking, often accompanied by a staff or board member. I have received many nice notes from CEOs thanking us for not "making them" ask people for money. A true Visionary Leader does not necessarily have to be the one to "pop the question" at an Ask visit. But it will mean a great deal to the donor to have them be present. Likewise, there is no substitute for an occasional phone call or e-mail from that CEO directly to the donor, just to update them on what's happening in the organization and to express genuine personal interest in how that donor is doing.

Once the team has seen the value of more CEO time spent on cultivation, a major reallocation of workloads often ensues. We have had many groups decide to restructure and add a COO to relieve the CEO of the daily management responsibility (which has often become tedious and unchallenging to a passionate Visionary Leader). Other groups choose to reallocate the work of their fund-development staff, perhaps moving a special-events person up into the role of Team Leader and elevating the former Team Leader to full-time major gifts. While this may sound like a costly use of resources, after several years of successful implementation, engaging more and more board members in the process, everyone sees the wisdom of making these "investments."

CHAPTER 15

REFINING YOUR SYSTEM OF EVENTS

As you get deeper into the implementation of the model, your attention will clearly shift to developing major donor relationships. You will have seen the value of everything you are doing. Most groups find they come to regard their existing special events in a new light. Either they are wonderful occasions to introduce or further cultivate donors, or they are events that have served their useful life and need to be "blessed and released."

In other words, it is time to put each of your existing events under the microscope and evaluate its role moving forward. Ultimately, if you choose to keep an event, it needs to have a very clear purpose and timeline, including a process for evaluating its efficacy each year so that it doesn't become unnecessarily entrenched.

AN IDEAL SYSTEM OF EVENTS

The ideal system of events we teach—which seems to be just about right for most groups—is made up of:
- A minimum of one Point of Entry per month
- One Ask Event per year
- Two Free Feel-Good Cultivation Events per year

Let's address these one at a time.

A Minimum of One Point of Entry Per Month

While one Point of Entry per month will keep the model going, most groups find, as they progress with the model, that they level off at one or two "official" Point of Entry Events per month at their office or center and then at least one "traveling" Point of Entry in a Box.

(Do not confuse these with the civic club presentations which are pre-Point of Entry Events.)

A Point of Entry in a Box is a true Point of Entry (including Facts, Emotion, and Capturing the Names with Permission) that is not held in your location. It may take place in a board member's conference room, rotate to various church halls of the many congregations your program works with, or be hosted in the living rooms of your supporters.

Imagine if you could actually take some of the events you are now working diligently to produce and turn them into your regularly scheduled Point of Entry Events, by inserting the three essential ingredients: Facts 101, the Emotional Hook, and being able to Capture the Names of the guests with their permission. You could jump-start your Point of Entry program without having to invent a whole new series of events.

Think about which of your existing events may already meet these requirements or could easily be modified to do so. The best contenders are well-attended, program-related events that repeat weekly or monthly; for example, tours, orientations, or open houses you may offer for new volunteers, staff, or members. Odds are, with only a bit of tweaking, you could have a ready-made Point of Entry.

The one criterion that is trickiest to meet is that the guests need to know in advance that they are coming to an introductory session about your organization, as opposed to coming to a more specific volunteer training, a lecture on a particular topic, an open house, or a fundraising event. For example, a retirement home we worked with had been holding regular Sunday afternoon open houses for family members and potential new residents. After adopting the Benevon Model, it was easy for them to add a thirty-minute sit-down Point of Entry "meeting." Rather than having to organize a whole new set of events, they merely added (and publicized) this more formal component to an already popular and well-attended event in their community.

No doubt, your organization has existing events that could qualify as natural Point of Entry Events, with only minor modifications. But what about all those other fundraising events you have been faithfully putting on: the golf tournaments and the galas? In our model, those have the potential to become what we call Point of Entry Conversion Events. Although these events are not nearly as efficient as official Point of Entry Events, when it comes to capturing permission to follow up and go further with each guest, they are great for reaching larger groups of (often new) people who might not otherwise have reason to learn about you. I like to think about them as pre-Point of Entry Events. It is fine to charge people money to come to a Point of Entry Conversion Event; just be sure that all of the objectives of a standard Point of Entry have been covered before they leave.

Here is a little test of whether your event qualifies as a Point of Entry for your guests: the next day, if someone asked them about the dinner-dance or the golf tournament, could the guests have answered the following two-question pop quiz?

Question 1: What was the name of the organization for which the event was raising funds?

While they may well remember how much they enjoyed the golf or the dinner-dance, will they be able to recall the name of the organization that worked so hard to produce the event and ultimately received their financial support?

Question 2: What does that organization do?

Even if your name is well known in your community, do not assume that people truly know about the breadth of your programs. What people will remember most is a short testimonial from someone who has benefited from your work.

In other words, you will need to insert a Point of Entry element into the sit-down portion of your fundraising event. This should include a short Visionary Leader Talk with facts and emotion, plus a brief, live testimonial from a person whose life has been changed thanks to the work of your organization. With good preparation, this can all be accomplished in ten minutes.

It almost goes without saying that you need to Capture the Names with the guests' permission. At most of these events, such as auctions or golf tournaments, you will have a natural way of knowing who will be coming in advance. Do not assume that this means you have their permission to follow up with them after the event.

Do you have good records of the names and phone numbers of the guests? Moreover, would you have a legitimate reason for calling them after the event to find out what they thought of it? Or would that seem too contrived? What could you add to the event that would let those guests who might want more information identify themselves so you would have sufficient permission to follow up with them?

For that explicit permission, you need to ask people at some point during the event if they would like you to contact them. The easiest way to do this is by placing a card under their lunch or dinner plate or in the center of their table. The emcee needs to refer to the card and encourage people to fill it out and leave it with their table host if they would like to speak directly with someone from the organization.

One Free One-Hour Ask Event Per Year

I do not recommend having more than one Ask Event per year, and for the most part, we forbid our groups from ever trying to convert any type of existing event into an Ask Event.

Some groups choose to put on more than one Ask Event the first year, recognizing that even if they meet our formulas for dollar results raised, their event will still not bring in enough first-year cash to meet their operating needs. Others choose to make their first Ask Event small to test it out quickly. Then, seeing success, they put on a larger event later in the same year. Most groups find, however, that once they get the rhythm of the model going smoothly, one Ask Event per year is plenty.

We also get groups trying to convince us that they are already putting on an event that is so similar to the Ask Event, it would be easier to convert their existing event than to design a new one. While that may be tempting, I do not recommend converting an existing event into a Free One-Hour Ask Event. It tends to upset people, especially if the event has been taking place for many years and people are accustomed to its format. The subtleties of the Free One-Hour Ask Event (no minimum gift required, no ticket price, asking for high dollar levels and five-year pledges) will be disconcerting to people. It's far better to start with a fresh event—ideally in the opposite season of the year—and have it become highly successful. Then you can decide what else to do with the older event: perhaps find a sponsor to cover the costs and convert it into a Free Feel-Good Cultivation Event.

Two Free Feel-Good Cultivation Events Per Year (Also Called Point of Re-Entry Events)

These wonderful events are not optional or frivolous in the model. In fact, we require our groups to have at least two of them per year. These events are strategically targeted at specific groups of prior donors in appreciation of their loyal support. They powerfully reconnect donors to the mission of the organization and reinforce their original decision to give. Just as with a Point of Entry, these events give people the Facts 101, the Emotional Hook, and a permission-based method for Capturing the Names. Donors leave feeling good and saying to themselves, "I'm glad I give money there. Maybe I could give more."

These insiders are always encouraged to bring friends to these Free Feel-Good Cultivation Events as well, so long as the focus of the event really is on your loyal prior donors. For the new people, the event will be a pre-Point of Entry Event. Just be sure to follow up to invite them to an official Point of Entry. Of course, just as with a Point of Entry, a Point of Re-Entry always engenders a Follow-Up Call, eliciting more feedback, which in turn enables you to further customize your approach to each donor. This keeps the donor going around the cycle with you.

Free Feel-Good Cultivation Events usually take on one of these four forms:

- **Traditional recognition events:** these popular, existing events include the awards dinner or more informal picnics, barbecues, or dinner parties in private homes.
- **Program or mission-related events:** the informal, but invitation-only, in-house program-related events, such as a special night for donors to serve soup in your soup kitchen or a special pre-graduation reception for Multiple-Year Donors.
- **Guest speakers:** the formal lectures or informal meetings with a celebrity scientist or artist on their newest work or discovery.

- **Briefings or "spinning the next dream:"** my personal favorite, because they pull back the curtain and let your donors know what the Visionary Leader is really grappling with: new challenges, program expansion, or upcoming capital or endowment campaigns.

Planning Your Free Feel-Good Cultivation Events Strategically

As you move into higher-level implementation of the model, I recommend you stratify your Free Feel-Good Cultivation Events for donors at different levels. This will keep them feeling very personal and improve attendance, which can sometimes be a challenge.

For example, you may invite your biggest donors to an elegant dinner at the most exclusive private home or with a revered person in your field, if that is the sort of thing they would like. Your smaller Multiple-Year Donors might be invited to a dinner, lecture series, family picnic, special "environmental day," or "peace day." Free Feel-Good Cultivation Events may also be used as Point of Entry Events to introduce insiders to the next dream for the organization, especially a major gifts campaign or endowment.

As for best times of year to hold these events, they are most often scheduled to occur about three months after your Ask Events, or else to coincide with natural program events such as arts performances, graduations, and holiday celebrations. Plan out each of these events well in advance and put them on your Master Cultivation Calendar.

Attendance at Free Feel-Good Cultivation Events

Not everyone will want to come to these events. Some people will be too busy, some don't like group events, and others will suspect you are going to ask them for more money. Recall that our Sustainable Funding Scorecard measure calls for two personal contacts for each Multiple-Year Donor. For some donors, that will look like having them attend two Free Feel-Good Cultivation Events per year. For others, it will be two one-on-one contacts (private meetings, phone calls, or private e-mail exchanges) per year. For some donors, it will be a mixture of both. That is why you need to have several options available.

SOUL-SEARCHING QUESTIONS

Hopefully, this discussion about events has sparked some new "a-ha!" moments. If you are serious about fully implementing the model, it is time to tell the truth about cutting out or modifying your existing fundraising events to keep your focus on growing the model.

Here are some soul-searching questions to ask as you consider refining your system of events:

1. Have you converted 100% of your prior "fundraising" events to Point of Entry Conversion Events?

Old-style fundraising events are not a part of this model. The fewer old-style fundraising events you have, the better. They can easily become a major distraction from the more important work of cultivating relationships with people who could become major donors. Take an unbiased inventory of your existing events and decide to either convert them to a Point of Entry or a Free Feel-Good Cultivation Event or do away with them altogether.

Having said that, most organizations have one or two big entertainment events that they want to keep. The fifteen-year-old black-tie gala that got started by one prominent couple or family may still be the place to be in your community. It would be silly to do away with it. In that case, figure out how to "missionize" the event and do thorough follow up afterwards. The golf tournament that was started by a corporate executive board member may take many more hours of work than the bottom line yields. Find a corporate sponsor to underwrite the entire event and even organize it for you with the golf club. You can go to the golf event to speak at the lunch or dinner banquet, if they are open to hearing about the work of your organization. Encourage people who are interested to fill out a card or give their business card to their table host if they would like to come to a Point of Entry.

2. Is there enough of an Emotional Hook at each of these events to ensure that the guests will never forget your organization?

Fancy centerpieces and pretty balloons are not what people remember. They remember the stories of your Testimonial Speakers and volunteers whose lives are being changed every day thanks to your work. Don't let people walk out of your events without having been truly moved by a human story.

3. Do you Capture the Names with Permission at these events?
Permission is one of the hallmarks of the model. Be sure you are only following up with people who gave you permission to do so. All your good work could be wasted with one annoying phone call or mailing that presumes people gave their permission for it. Think of how you like to be treated. Ask for permission and then do only what you were granted permission for.

4. Do you make a Follow-Up Call within one week to everyone who expressed an interest in learning more about your organization or coming to a Point of Entry?
Engage the person in a dialog. Try to discern which aspect of your work most piques their interest. If you are waiting longer than one week to follow up, you run the risk of people having forgotten the name of your group altogether. Schedule the Follow-Up Calls right into your event planning. The week or two after the event is by far the most fertile time to follow up with people.

Do you follow up again after that call to provide whatever next step the guest needs or wants? If the person requests more information about a particular program or wants to come to a Point of Entry, be sure to follow up in a timely manner (within one week) with an answer to their request. This serves to keep the dialog going. Use your tracking system to help you manage the timing of these calls or face-to-face meetings.

5. Do you have an airtight tickler system for ensuring this person will receive the regular personal contact they need as you move forward with the cultivation process?
Remember, this is the "science of special." Be sure you are communicating using their preferred method—e-mail, phone, or mail. As you get to know each person, you will learn their preferences and customize your contacts accordingly.

6. Do you have at least two Free Feel-Good Cultivation Events per year?
You need more than one, so your donors have a choice of the date and type of event. Even if they are not able to attend either event, the invitation affords you an opportunity to follow up and check in with them—another chance for a cultivation contact!

7. Are your Free Feel-Good Cultivation Events stratified so that one event is for your Multiple-Year Donors only?
One should be for your highest-level Multiple-Year Donors, perhaps held in a donor's home or as a special private meeting with a big name researcher or artist in the field. The other event can be for all of your Multiple-Year Donors. Ideally, these are events you would be having anyway, like graduation ceremonies, kids' art night at school, or your summer camp's annual visiting day.

HOW TO PHASE OUT AN EXISTING EVENT

In the process of asking these soul-searching questions, many groups come to realize that it is time to phase out a popular (or not-so-popular) event. If the decision were theirs alone to make, they would know how to eliminate it. But events tend to build up loyal followers and supporters, often for emotional (and no longer rational) reasons. The best way to eliminate an event is to do an analysis of what it costs versus what it yields and then do a phase-out plan, retaining the best aspects of the event or inserting them into other events you are keeping.

In other words, do your homework. Put together the spreadsheets showing the true costs associated with putting on the event, including the hidden staff time and the opportunity cost of having staff focus on this event rather than on other major gifts work. Document the results that have come from the event. Propose how to capitalize on the best parts of the event—the sponsors and some of the key guests—and connect them even more to your mission. Explain how streamlining the event will give you time to do proper follow up. Present all this to the executive director and the people on the board who will be most supportive of eliminating the event. Secure their buy-in before taking it to the full board (if necessary).

For example, we have a group that had a fancy awards banquet to honor donors and volunteers, and it was underwritten with corporate tables. The event had become quite stale. Most guests had no connection to the organization or the award recipients. They were given a "ticket" from their boss and told to attend. While some of these people could have become interested in the organization during the event, that was unlikely without a large dose of the mission to educate and inspire them. That is tricky to do at a fancy banquet.

Rather than keep this event going as is, they converted it into a Free Feel-Good Cultivation Event for all of their Multiple-Year Donors, making it special and free for them to attend. They made sure that the award recipients showcased the various program areas of the organization, using stories about each program in the actual award presentation. They restructured their program to include a brief Visionary Leader Talk and a testimonial from a person whose life had been changed thanks to their work. The total program lasted thirty minutes and left people inspired and educated about their work. They reduced the number of sponsors down to one so that it was a special privilege to be the sponsor of this event, with more visibility and a more exclusive audience. Then they asked some of the other prior banquet sponsors to sponsor their other events, such as other Point of Entry Conversion Events like their golf tournament—which they decided to keep doing—as well as their Ask Event.

Even if you see that you need to eliminate several events, I recommend that you design a two- to three-year phase-out plan so you can test out the impact of each one as you continue to show results over time with the model—both from your Ask Event and the other one-on-one major gifts asking you will be doing. That way, when you are ready to phase out the third or fourth event, critics will have seen the impact of the model. In the worst case, you will decide to keep these other events, and the board will see the importance of hiring someone else to manage them, freeing you up to keep focusing on growing the model towards sustainable funding.

CHAPTER 16

BUILDING A SUSTAINABLE TEAM

Now that you see how much work is involved in keeping the model alive and fresh within your organization, you can also see how important it is to have a strong team of people to manage and carry out the implementation going forward and a system for ensuring that team can sustain itself.

I want to be sure to put an end to any of the self-implementers out there, including those of you who have been senior major gifts people in large, well-established organizations who feel you already "know how to do this." While it may seem like you are perfectly capable of doing all the steps yourself, at least for the first year, I believe it truly does a disservice to a nonprofit organization—long term—not to engage more people in the process right from the start. In other words, whether or not you ever attend any of our programs, if you are serious about building sustainable funding for an organization you love, please don't do it alone.

We have seen many a superstar development person or major gifts officer adopt the model wholeheartedly—without ever getting the deeper buy-in of the executive director, CEO, board, or other key volunteers. It is painful to watch how hard that person works, even with good financial success the first year.

The second year is where we see these superstars become frustrated. Because the others in the organization don't understand the four steps of the circular model, the richness and robustness of the model will quickly devolve to an annual Ask Event, and that wonderful lone implementer, who was so interested in carrying this forward, will move on.

If the sole implementer leaves, no one will be left behind to cultivate and involve your new Multiple-Year Donors so they will stay with you for years to come. No one will be there to expand the reach of your Point of Entry Events to other groups within the community. Rather than nurturing the process so that it becomes a strong, deeply-rooted, fruit-bearing tree, the low-hanging fruit will have been picked, and the tree will be left un-watered.

BUILDING YOUR SUSTAINABLE FUNDING DREAM TEAM

If you don't yet have a team or if you have been tolerating a weak team, now is the time to start building your dream team. This type of "fundraising" requires a very different team than traditional event planners or major gifts solicitors. The job description for these team members focuses on building one-on-one relationships with donors and tending those relationships over time. Groups often refer to this as their Sustainable Funding Team.

Initially, this is a cross-functional team of five to seven people: staff, board, and volunteers. Most organizations do not have such a team already in place. The nearest they come to having a team is the development committee composed of busy board members who did not sign on for this model. A mixed team made up of the executive director, development director, board chair or vice chair, board development committee chair, and three "roll-up-your-sleeves" community volunteers represents a broader cross-section and will be more stable. As turnover naturally occurs, people can be replaced with others from that same category. And, as we have seen, if the model is implemented properly, it will generate many new, passionate people who ask to become involved—people who would be excellent team members.

Do not be concerned if your organization doesn't have people in one of these categories—for example, if you don't have any paid staff, you can balance out your team between the groups you do have, such as board members and volunteers.

Staffing

Most groups find that after their success with the model the first year, they are ready to invest to grow it deeper within the organization. They usually commit to allocating one full-time staff person to coordinating the implementation of the model in the second year. This person becomes the Team Leader, overseeing the entire model, including managing the critical Point of Entry process.

If this is to be a paid staff position, it does not necessarily need to be a new staff member. Priorities may have shifted so that staff assignments can be reallocated—for example, spending time on some of the more labor-intensive fundraising activities that have been consuming your staff may seem less productive now.

Over time, as the model grows, you will see the need to expand your team. I'd recommend you aim for a structure with one overall Team Leader and sub-teams (or at least sub-team members) to focus on each of the four steps of the model. The diagram below shows one possible structure for a group in its fourth year of using the model.

SUSTAINABLE FUNDING TEAM

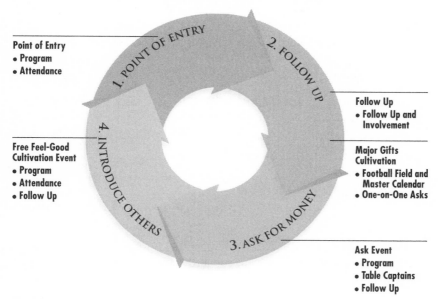

Point of Entry
- Program
- Attendance

1. POINT OF ENTRY

2. FOLLOW UP

Follow Up
- Follow Up and Involvement

Major Gifts Cultivation
- Football Field and Master Calendar
- One-on-One Asks

4. INTRODUCE OTHERS

Free Feel-Good Cultivation Event
- Program
- Attendance
- Follow Up

3. ASK FOR MONEY

Ask Event
- Program
- Table Captains
- Follow Up

There is one overall Sustainable Funding Team Leader. Then, in this example, there are eleven team members each focused on one of the bulleted areas.

Under Point of Entry Events, there are two team members, one in charge of the Point of Entry Program itself and the second in charge of attendance at the Point of Entry Events.

Under Follow Up and Involvement, there is one person in charge of this whole area. This person may well have a small group of volunteers who assist with the Follow-Up Calls, especially after the Ask Event when there are many more calls to be made.

Under Ask Event, there is one person in charge of the day-of-event program, one in charge of Table Captains, who will likely have several people reporting to them, and one in charge of Ask Event Follow Up. This Ask Event Follow-Up person may rely on the Follow-Up Call volunteers from Step Two of the model.

Under Free Feel-Good Cultivation Events, we have three sub-team leaders. One leader is in charge of the program at the Free Feel-Good Cultivation Event. This involves arranging the Testimonial Speaker and the Visionary Leader Talk. One leader is in charge of ensuring good attendance at the event and making sure that everyone receives a personal invitation whether or not they choose to attend. And, of course, another leader is responsible for following up after the event.

You'll note also, a fifth team for Major Gifts Cultivation. On this team, we have one person in charge of tracking all of the football fields in process and coordinating all next-action steps on one master calendar. Finally, there is one person who oversees the one-on-one Asks, making sure that they actually happen!

Choosing Team Members

We spend a great deal of time helping groups put together an effective team. I don't think we have ever had a group call us and say they already have a perfect team in place. Rather, most groups initially feel they do not have five to seven people who would want to be involved with this, regardless of whether they are board members, staff, or volunteers.

This feeling is normal, so don't be discouraged. Look over your group's Treasure Map for possible team members who are right under your nose. Former board members are my first choice for the ideal team member. If they were strong, contributing board members for many years, who loved telling other people about your work and left in good standing, their passion is likely still there for the organization.

Serving on the Sustainable Funding Team is a different type of commitment than serving on the board. Rather than carrying the responsibility of governing and overseeing the entire operation, a team member needs to be an ambassador for your organization in the community. So choose people who love talking about your organization and who are naturally going to do that, whether they are on your board or not. Choose people who are upbeat, fun to work with, organized, and who do what they say they will do. Choose the people who will enjoy doing this and won't need a lot of tending. Think long-term sustainability: choose the people you would trust to carry the model forward even after you are gone.

TEAM MEMBER JOB DESCRIPTION

The specific responsibilities of each team member will vary depending on that person's role on the team as well as their interests and strengths. As a whole, the responsibilities of most team members include:

1. Learning the Benevon Model (online, book, or introductory session).
2. Attending at least one Point of Entry Event and bringing five or more friends each year.
3. Hosting a Point of Entry Event.
4. Making a personal Treasure Map twice a year and adding the names to the list of potential Point of Entry attendees.
5. Making thank-you and invitation calls as requested.
6. Being a Table Captain at the Ask Event and filling a table with nine other people.
7. Attending Free Feel-Good Cultivation Events and bringing others.

8. Taking on other special roles on the team as desired (being a greeter at Point of Entry Events, etc.).

Time Commitment

What sort of time commitment will this take? The first year, we say it takes an average of twenty hours per week for a team of five to seven people to collectively implement the model, so the average member can expect to spend two to four hours per week on this.

That being said, the twenty hours per week your team spends on implementing the model will probably not be divided evenly among the team members. Some will do more in the beginning—perhaps they will plan and manage the Point of Entry Events. Others may be involved in the middle of the process, in the Follow Up and Cultivation phase of the model, and others may step up for the Ask Event or for the ongoing tending of your new donors.

As the process evolves, team members may increase (or decrease) their level of involvement. Do not be surprised when team members become reconnected to the work of the organization and take on a greater role on the team.

Start by asking for a minimum of a one-year commitment to serve on the team. That is as much as most people will be willing to commit to, at first. But let people know that you hope they will become so engaged in the process that they will want to stay longer.

Groups in our longer-term programs have team members who have been with them for upwards of five years, including long-time CEOs and current and former board members. Once the team has defined their game plan to achieve sustainable funding, people see a clear pathway and the steps to be taken. They want to stick around to be part of the process.

Much like the Ask Event donor who makes a personal choice to make a multiple-year pledge, these team members re-commit at a more personal level to be part of the team. And that attracts others. Rather than struggling to fill an empty "slot" on a team, you will be blessed with an abundance of wonderful contenders. After all, who wouldn't want to be part of a winning team that supports the fulfillment of a mission they are most passionate about?

CHOOSING THE TEAM LEADER

The Team Leader has a unique role—to coordinate the team's efforts, not to do all the work! We recommend that the Team Leader be the person who is responsible for the fund development process within the organization. Usually this is a paid staff member, ideally the development director, if the organization has one.

The biggest challenge for Team Leaders is to delegate tasks to people who are often higher in the organization's hierarchy, such as their executive director or esteemed board members.

If the team meets regularly to update their progress, people's enthusiasm builds, and people naturally take on parts of the process that they enjoy. Ideally, then the Team Leader functions more like a conductor of an orchestra. The key is starting with team members who really want to be on the team and who really care about the organization.

The Team Leader's responsibilities include:

- Coordinating and implementing the organization's annual fundraising plan.
- Managing the team to meet deadlines and complete assigned tasks.
- Ensuring that all data is captured in the database tracking system.
- Personally taking on or delegating all tasks needed to fulfill each element of the fundraising plan.
- When the time comes, recruiting and grooming the next Team Leader.

KEEPING TEAM MEMBERS PASSIONATE AND FEELING APPRECIATED

The best way to keep your team members feeling connected is to make sure they attend one of your sizzling Point of Entry Events at least once a year. While some of the team will naturally be involved in putting on your Point of Entry Events, and therefore will be attending them often, others may be more removed. Make sure they have the pleasure of witnessing your work in action.

Ask team members to talk about their experiences with their fellow board members, staff, or volunteers. Have them help you talk up the process. Showcase their work at board meetings, volunteer appreciation events, and certainly at your Ask Event. While recognition is not the main reason your team members are participating, everyone appreciates being thanked, and it will inspire others to get involved.

TURNOVER: BUILDING A SELF-SUSTAINING TEAM

Over time, our groups have streamlined the team member job responsibilities to spread the work and continuously bring in new talent. For example, one team has a sub-team captain for each step of the model—one team captain in charge of Point of Entry Events, one in charge of follow up, one in charge of the Ask Event, and one in charge of cultivation and one-on-one asking. That way, as new, qualified, passionate people come forward, they can groom them as team members or sub-team captains, so there is an ongoing plan for refreshing the team and allowing people to step off after several years of service, if they so choose.

The best time to plan for those transitions is after each year's Ask Event. Meet as a team to celebrate your success and debrief the year's results and lessons learned. Look ahead to the next phase of implementation—be it cultivation, asking for major gifts, or planning Free Feel-Good Cultivation Events. Ask people how they would like to be involved moving forward. Encourage people to stay on the team, so they can have the satisfaction of seeing the model grow over time.

This is also the time to "bless and release" those who do not want to continue in a formal role on your team. Be sure to find out how they would like to stay involved, for example as VIP guests at your Ask Event.

Do not default to the scarcity mentality as some of your team members naturally cycle off the team. If you have been following the model diligently, you'll be able to refresh your team with some of the passionate new people the model will have attracted—including new board members.

CHAPTER 17

ENGAGING YOUR BOARD

Most groups tell us there is a direct correlation between their success with the model and the level of engagement of their board members. In other words, as the model takes hold and grows roots in the daily life of your organization, you should naturally find your current (and former) board members becoming more involved and more excited, or they should be offering to step off the board to make room for new people who may have been introduced to your organization at a Point of Entry or an Ask Event and want to become more involved—at the board level. This is a good thing.

Much has been written and said about the roles for board members today—their fiduciary responsibilities, effective models for board governance, etc. The Benevon Model is not designed to change any of that. Clearly, the board's first role is to govern the organization. Yet that is often not how it feels to board members. To board members, fundraising usually feels like their first (and often most dreaded) responsibility.

Much has also been written and said about roles for board members when it comes to fundraising. Usually this focuses on the traditional annual fund or major gifts campaign strategy, whereby board members identify potential donors, who are usually friends and colleagues, for the organization to write letters to and solicit in person.

Many organizations aspire to have such a "fundraising board," either because they think they are supposed to have that, or because they think it would handle their fundraising needs forever. They berate themselves for not having such a "fundraising board." I refer to this as "board envy," and it is not rooted in any reality I have ever seen.

If you pull back the curtain from those well-established organizations with "fundraising boards" that are the envy of every other group, you will find a team of dedicated, hard-working staff who coordinate the process of strategically cultivating each donor and engaging volunteer board members at every step of the way, including the ultimate Ask.

The fantasy of the magical fundraising board that will do all the work and raise all the money is a myth. Those organizations have a systematic plan for how they grow and cultivate relationships with donors. They certainly don't rely on their board members to save the day.

While we work with many groups that have well-established fundraising programs, including groups that are already raising many millions of dollars each year before they come to our workshops, they often tell us they still do not feel they have a system for keeping their board members engaged. They experience board burnout and turnover, just like the small and mid-sized organizations do. They use our model as a mission-centered strategy for ongoing donor—and board—engagement.

If you are truly committed to leaving the legacy of self-sustaining funding, there is no better place to start than with your board. Rather than distracting your focus and wasting time comparing your board to others, get to work on specific strategies for keeping your board engaged.

THE BENEVON GOLDEN RULE

Above all, treat your board members as if they will become your most cherished major donors. That sounds simple, but when you scan through the list of your board members one by one—if you tell the truth—there may be a few members who you've already written off in your mind, either because they are annoying or troublesome to you in some way, or because you have predetermined that they do not have the capacity to become a major donor. That is a violation of the Golden Rule.

Think about your list of major donors, at whatever dollar level you define as "major." Think of all the special things you do or try to do for those donors—special events, letters, calls, and meetings. Think about the respect and humility you bring to each interaction, regardless of that donor's quirky personality. You have a great deal of tolerance for your donors, knowing their capacity to give.

Why, then, do groups discriminate when it comes to their board members? These are people who are giving their own time to do something you invited them to do, to serve on your board. That is a great gift unto itself.

Furthermore, the statistics show that 90% of people who volunteer in America also give money. That doesn't mean they necessarily give money to the same organizations where they volunteer. It just means that "volunteering" people are also "giving" types of people.

And here, in your board members, you have the most dedicated volunteers. Why not assume they will become your most passionate major donors? Even if they do not have the capacity to give a large gift now, odds are they will be making charitable gifts either now or at the end of their lives to one or more organizations.

Where else would they rather give that money than to an organization that has treated them well throughout the years—an organization whose work they know and love and perhaps has benefited them or their families personally?

What systems do you have for cultivating and engaging your major donors? You have a plan for talking to them several times a year, personally and face-to-face. You invite them to selected mission-focused Free Feel-Good Cultivation Events each year. You consciously continue to deepen your relationship with them, finding out at every opportunity how else they might like to become involved, what more they need from the organization, and who else they might want to introduce.

These are the same sorts of systems you will want to put in place for your board members!

THREE ROLES FOR BOARD MEMBERS

The fastest route to sanity and satisfaction is to accept the 20-60-20 rule when it comes to fundraising and your board members. That is, 20% of the board will enjoy being involved in fundraising, 60% will be neutral about it, and the remaining 20% will want nothing to do with it.

For those board members who want to help with fundraising, there are three easy ways they can participate and make an even greater contribution to your organization:

- **Invite people to Point of Entry Events.** If your board members did nothing more than this, they would be making an enormous contribution to the future of your organization. They can agree to be the board member "host of the month" for a regularly-scheduled Point of Entry Event and then invite a few people to attend that event. Or they can agree to host a private event, just for their friends, business colleagues, civic group, etc.

- **Thank donors for gifts.** Ask your board members to telephone individual donors just to thank them. Not all board members will want to do this, but once a few of them report on how wonderful the experience was at the next board meeting, others may offer to jump in.

- **Give money themselves.** You need to be able to tell your community that 100% of your board gives money personally to your organization, regardless of the amount. Many board members will make their gift at the annual Ask Event. Others may choose to be part of a pooled Leadership or Challenge Gift. If you treat each board member as if they will become your most cherished major donor, over time you will naturally know how to work with each board member individually. (Note that we are aiming here for personal gifts from each board member, which may be in addition to a gift from their corporation.)

TOP TEN CHECKLIST:
INVOLVING YOUR BOARD

How does your board stack up? Here is a series of questions for telling the truth about how you are doing at involving your board.

1. When it comes to fundraising, what are your biggest concerns about your board? What more would you like your board members to be doing? What would it take for your board to more closely resemble your image of the "ideal" board?

2. What percentage of your total board members would you rate as truly passionate about your work? Do the math. The sooner you tell the truth about this percentage, the sooner you can get to work.

3. What percentage of your total board members understand the Benevon Model and are eager to participate in its implementation? Notice, this is not asking how many have heard of the model or nod their heads pleasantly when you discuss Point of Entry Events and the Ask Event, but rather what percentage truly understand the power of the model to build long-term sustainable funding—something most board members would love to leave as a legacy.

4. What percentage of total board members have attended a Point of Entry?

5. More importantly, what percentage of your board members have invited others to attend Point of Entry Events? Some groups make this a standard part of board participation, going so far as to have board members sign an agreement to attend at least one Point of Entry per year and to have a minimum number of guests throughout the year.

6. What percentage of your board members have been involved in thanking donors? What have they said about it afterwards? Are they sharing their enthusiasm about doing this at board meetings?

7. What percentage of your board members give money to the organization? Your goal here should be 100% participation, with no minimum dollar requirement

8. Do you do a Treasure Map Interview with each board member once a year? These simple Treasure Map Interview questions (see Chapter 8) are very powerful. If your CEO and board chair were to do an annual Treasure Map Interview with each of your board members, that would send a powerful message that each board member is very important to you.

   It would give your board members an opportunity to talk to you and, even more importantly, give you an opportunity to listen to them, which again sends the message that you value them. Furthermore, if you pay close attention to what they are telling you in these annual Treasure Map Interviews, you will see what has changed in their life circumstances and priorities in the past year, what lights them up most about your work, and how you can involve them in precisely those areas.

9. What is your plan to increase or retread your board members' passion? This new level of engagement for each board member isn't going to happen automatically. It takes someone to drive it, step by step.

   Just as you would develop a "football field" for cultivating each major donor, you need a similar step-by-step plan for cultivating each board member. This won't be a mystery. It is a function of personalized contacts, each focusing on the board member's particular area of interest—be it your diabetes-prevention program or the day nursery for babies born with HIV.

You'd be arranging private meetings for your board members with the heads of those programs or letting them visit your work in action. It would all be customized to precisely what they asked for.

Each subsequent contact would be driven by the board member's request during a prior contact. Those particular interests would be the things you'd want to be engaging your board member in—according to the pace and timing this board member most prefers. You need a plan for engaging your board members, just like you need a plan for cultivating major donors.

10. Have you given your board members specific ways to be involved in the Benevon process? For example, do you make it easy for your board members to invite people to attend your Point of Entry Events? Some groups give board members business cards printed with the dates of upcoming Point of Entry Events to hand out to friends in the course of each month.

    Have you asked each board member to host a Point of Entry by inviting a few friends and formally welcoming people at the start of the program? This also lets other board members know that, even if they are unable to personally attend the event, the friends they are inviting will be greeted warmly by a board member.

    Other groups ask one board member to volunteer to make thank-you phone calls to donors each month. This becomes a real Passion Retread exercise for the board members. Listening to happy donors say why they appreciate the work of your organization reconnects board members to their own passion.

    Regarding the Ask Event, have you asked each board member to be a Table Captain or host a VIP table at the Ask Event?

ANNUAL BOARD FUNDRAISING RETREAT

To keep the model fresh as board members come and go, I recommend you hold an annual board fundraising retreat. Here is the proposed agenda for this retreat.

BOARD RETREAT SAMPLE AGENDA (90 MINUTES)

1. Welcome and Introductions	Board Chair	5 min.
2. Do a Passion Retread: have each board member say why they chose to volunteer with the organization.	Executive Director/ Board Chair	15 min.
3. Explain the Benevon Model or show the Benevon video or DVD and show where your organization is on the cycle.	Development Director	20 min.
4. Have a board member state your goal to implement the entire model culminating with an Ask Event on _____ (date). To do that, you will need to have _____ (number of) Point of Entry guests by _____ (date). Show them your strategy/plan and where you plan to focus, e.g., prior donors, alumni, others in the community.	Board Member	5 min.
5. Make a quick Treasure Map with the board (or walk them through the one you have already done). Show them the list of potential Table Captains you have developed, including some of them.	Team Leader	15 min.
6. Have each board member make a personal Treasure Map and identify at least fifteen people they could invite to a Point of Entry or Ask Event.	Team Leader	10 min.
7. Discussion/Q & A	Executive Director	20 min.

Let's walk through this agenda step by step, because it includes several critical elements that can be used at other times of the year as well.

The first item on the agenda sets the tone. It is what we call the Passion Retread exercise. It is easy to do, non-threatening, and guaranteed to connect people to their passion for your work—and to each other—very quickly. That's why we put it first on the agenda. Once people are in touch with why they are giving their time to your group, they have a great deal more compassion for one another and can focus more on the work at hand.

Ask people: "What is so special about the work of this organization that makes you want to give your time to it? What is it about this place that attracted you in the first place, and what keeps you here now?"

As your board members share their reasons for involvement, you'll find that some of the stories are very personal and moving, while others may be amusing. As the stories spill out, members of the group will rediscover their connection to the organization. At the same time, participants will gain a deeper respect for and connection to each other. People come to appreciate—and be more tolerant of—the quirky or challenging members of the group.

In the end, all who participate in this exercise will have new energy and enthusiasm for telling the story of the organization to the community. They will be reminded of just how important the work of this organization is and why they want to help out.

Next take fifteen to twenty minutes to explain how the model works. More and more, our groups are having this part of the agenda presented by a board member or former board member who is enthusiastic about mission-centered fundraising and sees the long-term merit of the model.

An alternative to this is showing them our free online video or DVD. Be sure to highlight how you have customized the model. Tell your board members the name of your Point of Entry and show them where the Ask Event lives on the cycle, so that they see it is just one step in a four-step circular process that spirals up to major gifts and endowment.

Next, share your goals—both short- and long-term—using the model. Tell them the date of your next Ask Event and, using our formulas, the number of Point of Entry guests you will need to have by a specific date.

Finally, make a quick Treasure Map (see Appendix for instructions). Let them identify groups in the community they feel would want to know you better. Choose the four groups on the Treasure Map you plan to focus on for Point of Entry guests and ultimately for Table Captains. Show them the list of potential Table Captains you have developed.

Have each board member make a personal Treasure Map of the people in their lives who would naturally want to attend your Point of Entry. Ask them to make a list of at least fifteen of those people. This list can become their guest list if they agree to be a Table Captain at the Ask Event.

While this is best done in a group, if a new board member joins your board shortly after you have held this retreat, you can meet with them in their home or office to walk them through the same process. Be sure to have them make a personal Treasure Map (see Appendix for more on this). When combined with the many groups on your organization's Treasure Map, these personal Treasure Maps of your board members, collectively, could fill many Point of Entry Events and one large Ask Event.

THE ADVISORY COMMITTEE AND THE HONORARY ADVISORY COMMITTEE

Advisory committees have been around for years, usually relegated to occasional special projects. Rarely, in my experience, have they been truly consulted for advice.

Two roles for these committees bear mentioning if you are considering starting an advisory committee or wondering how to better utilize the one you have.

First, as more and more national nonprofits consolidate their total number of chapters down to as few as one chapter per state or region, the stature of local advisory committees will be elevated. The statewide or regional oversight chapter will need to rely on these local advisory committees more to tap into the pulse and resources of the local community. This is their real value.

If you are fortunate enough to have an advisory committee, let them advise you! There is no substitute for listening to local people—ideally representing diverse points of view. And when it comes to fundraising, donors give locally first. These advisory committees may need to take a more active role in the fundraising process. Much of what has already been discussed in this book as fundraising roles for boards will naturally flow to these advisory committees as well.

I have seen the model work beautifully in a statewide organization that had only one governing board. Their fourteen local advisory committees hosted monthly Point of Entry Events and annual Ask Events in each community, yielding great results.

A second role for advisory committees and honorary advisory committees is as a place for grooming people for positions on the governing board and, if desired, for elevating the stature of the governing board or transitioning several board members at once. This is a bit more sensitive topic.

I am a big fan of honorary advisory committees, and I predict they will become more popular, especially given how hard it can be to get top people to commit to serving on the governing board of a nonprofit. The honorary advisory committee lets them give you their advice, which is what you really want, and connect you to people they feel could help you. This committee can meet a few times a year or not at all.

It takes work to keep these people connected, but if you have a diligent development director and executive director/CEO, this can be an incredibly productive use of time. Make your list of the five or six people whose advice you would really love to have and, working through a mutual acquaintance (ideally one of your board members), approach them about becoming an honorary advisory committee member. Invite them to a Point of Entry, and tell them you'd like to

meet with them in person at their office or another convenient location, one-on-one, four times a year. Then be prepared with questions
you really need answers to. Let them do the talking, and thank them
for their time.

Over time, depending on their level of engagement, some may
be willing to join your regular board, especially if they know that
some of the other honorary advisory committee members (whom
they respect) have agreed to do so also.

TO SUMMARIZE

Keeping your board engaged and refreshed is an ongoing process
that won't just happen on its own. If you think of this process like
the cultivation—nurturing and tending—of each of your precious
major donors, the experience and results will be much more satisfying for everyone.

CHAPTER 18

SUSTAINABLE FUNDING ON YOUR DESKTOP—HAVING A TRACKING SYSTEM YOU LOVE

Your organization's donor database is the collective institutional memory of the entire cultivation process with each donor. Long after your staff, board, and volunteers have moved on, that database will live on, full of the rich details of each cultivation contact and each Ask.

Rather than regard the database as a burden or annoyance or something to be "managed" by someone who is peripheral to the process, I recommend you design it to be something each team member can trust enough to rely on as their personal memory bank, diary, or journal, chronicling every single step of the process. In other words, consider that your tracking system could be something you love.

Furthermore, if it is properly secured, easy to use, readily accessible to everyone on your team, and linked to a calendar function, it can become an easy and natural way to communicate updates on donor contacts, manage the next contacts for each donor, and manage your overall cultivation calendar as well.

I clearly recall, way back in 1992, purchasing the first database for our school with my own money. I knew then that if I was going to be successful as the sole staff member working on fundraising, a great database would be essential. Most of my days were spent sitting at a little desk in front of my computer screen with my headset on, making phone calls to supporters and donors, reconfirming with Point of Entry guests, making Follow-Up Calls, and tracking every single conversation in that database. Long after I left there, subsequent development directors at the school thanked me for setting up that database and for the quality and detail of my notes, which taught them the importance of entering such critical information.

In other words, your database is a huge part of your legacy. Even after your group has successfully achieved all of your initial financial goals, you will need that collective repository for future generations.

Back then, in the early 1990s, just having a computer database of any type was considered very progressive. Plus, I was pretty much working alone. So one person, one desktop computer, and one software package made sense. Fast-forward to today, and I would certainly recommend something Web-based that everyone on your team can use. It's ideal to have a database that functions more like a private Web site for your team, where everyone can enter their notes, check on the status of various "football fields," and assign next steps after every single contact to ensure that no donor is left to fall between the cracks.

Several years ago, we set out to find such software that we could recommend to our groups and came upon eTapestry, which we have partnered with to design an inexpensive private-label version for our model. Here is a listing of what that Web-based software allows you to track. Whether you choose to use our product or another one, if you are serious about implementing the model, your donor relationship software needs to meet all of the following requirements.

TRACKING SYSTEM REQUIREMENTS

- Tracks relationships and contacts over time, not just basic contact information and gift history
- Easy to use by everyone on your team
- Interfaces with your Web site, so that Web site information is captured directly into the database
- Delivers and stores individual and mass e-mail
- Provides a log of contacts
- Integrates with your calendar and tickler system, so that all notes have dates and action items that link to appropriate date in daily planner
- Tracks relationships between people

- Tracks which events people attended (when invited and by whom)
- Tracks which mailings/contacts people responded to
- Tracks Follow-Up Call dates, messages left, and what was said on the call (ideally, the Follow-Up Call form is included in database and answers can just be filled in there)

To summarize, your tracking system should be the one solid, reliable repository for the chronology of every contact with each donor, potential donor, and volunteer. That is the only way everyone who has access to your database will come to count on this as the sole source for up-to-the-minute information on each donor.

CHAPTER 19

MOVING FORWARD
TO SUSTAINABILITY—
THE THREE "A-HA!" MOMENTS

Step back and think about that legacy you are aiming to leave. Those ten-year goals you wrote down in Chapter 2, on the Our Legacy of Sustainable Funding Worksheet. Where do you want to be by then? Will you have completed a capital campaign and be well on your way toward a sizable endowment? How many new major donors will you have added? What other goals will have been met: new board members, community awareness of your mission, or new programs added? What will the pathway really look like between here and there?

We find there comes a rollover moment for most groups we train and coach, usually about the third year. By then, they have won over enough of their internal skeptics and naysayers, seen many of the pieces of the model come together, and experienced enough financial success.

At this point they seem to experience three "a-ha!" moments.

First comes the "a-ha!" about Point of Entry Events. They realize that rather than having to force a formal event every month, looking under rocks to find guests to attend them, they can easily convert many of their existing events into Point of Entry Events. In fact, whether they become official Point of Entry Events or not, every single event they are now doing is an opportunity to insert a "Point-of-Entry-like experience" for each guest. Though they may not officially be able to Capture the Names and do the proper Follow-Up Calls, at least they have shifted away from needing to entertain people 100% of the time and have moved towards connecting people to their mission. They realize that they would rather put their limited time and energy into finding those donors who really want to stay with them long-term. They also realize that entertaining people is not a way to find out if they really love your mission.

A second "a-ha!" comes after several successes with major gift Asks. It is all about cultivation. I recently received a nice e-mail from one of our superstar CEOs, thanking us for the cultivation and Ask practice we had done with her team at our recent Major Gifts Lab. She said, "Thanks to all that football field work and that practice asking we did with you there, we went out and asked that donor, and just today we got a $3 million gift from him!" She went on to say, "If anyone ever doubts the efficacy of this model, just send them to me!"

Another of our outstanding Visionary Leader executive directors called us after securing another million-dollar gift and said, "I only wish we had started with this model years ago so that we would have more well-cultivated donors in the pipeline right now—more people who love our mission that we could be asking for these big gifts."

This is the rollover moment, when people begin to relax and trust the model. Now, having a few solid successes in their bank accounts, they see in hindsight that every single contact they've been having with each donor or potential donor has been a contact on the Cultivation Superhighway, going all the way back to the first Point of Entry or even earlier (to that first college acceptance letter).

They realize that this level of cultivation and asking is truly not very hard and, if systematized, it can become (to put it rather bluntly) a "numbers game."

This is when they have the third "a-ha!" They see that, if they just take the time to educate and inspire people, "bless and release" those who are not interested in going further, and tend and nurture those who make ever-increasing multiple-year gifts, all the while focusing relentlessly on the goalpost—sustainable funding—their group (*your* group) can be just as successful as any major university or other highly professional major gifts program.

And remember, those universities don't stop with major gifts. They are aiming for endowment funds to under-gird and sustain them for the future. This same dream can be fulfilled for any nonprofit that is willing to do the work—systematically—to make it happen.

CREATING A TREASURE MAP

Excerpted from "Raising More Money—The Point of Entry Handbook"

As you begin to see the merit of Point of Entry Events, you will naturally wonder who to invite to them. Given the personal nature of this model, it only makes sense to start with the people who already are connected to you in some way. You can branch out from there, following the stream of passion and natural word-of-mouth connections that link people. Before you know it, the whole system will snowball.

Rather than spending time trying to interest the obvious wealthy donors in your community who may not know or care about your organization, take the time to brainstorm about the natural supporters who are lurking right under your nose. We use the term "Treasure Map" because it identifies the natural treasure around you right now. You don't have to go out of your way to find these people. You don't have to make your selections based on wealth or social status. Include everyone and brainstorm away.

Learning to Draw a Treasure Map

This brainstorming exercise is best done with a team of people—ideally, the same team that will be involved in implementing the model over the next year or two. The more diverse your team members, the more diverse the Treasure Map. At some point, you will want to do this exercise with your board as well. If you are the person who will be leading the group through the process, be sure to practice it first with a small group of staff members, family, or friends.

Get out a large piece of paper and colored markers and lead your team through the process. Begin by drawing a circle in the center of the page. Put the name of your organization in the circle.

Then surround your organization, like the spokes on a wheel, with all of the other groups you come in contact with on a regular basis. Start with groups like your board, staff, volunteers, donors and funders, vendors, and other groups in the community that you interact with regularly.

TREASURE MAP
GROUPS AND ORGANIZATIONS

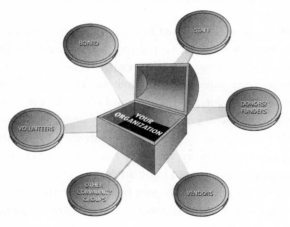

You may be able to subdivide groups like your board or staff further into former board, former board presidents, founding board members, etc. Similarly, your volunteers may be subdivided by the type of projects they are involved with. United Way, for example, has many substrata of loaned executive volunteers—depending on the industry they came from or the industry they will be soliciting. Red Cross volunteers may be subcategorized as blood volunteers, disaster volunteers, health and safety volunteers, and so on.

Take the time to brainstorm as many groups as you can think of. You can lump all the civic groups under one category. All the other community organizations you interact with may be a group or you may choose to subdivide them into categories like law enforcement, schools, other arts organizations, etc.

The more detail you can put into the Treasure Map as you list these groups, the more you will be able to target their specific resources and self-interests in the later steps of the Treasure Map process.

Resources in Abundance

Now, with a differently colored pen or marker, list the resources which each of these groups has in abundance. Why? Because this is an abundance-based model of fundraising. It presumes people will naturally want to give that which they have plenty of.

Most of us do not like saying no; it makes us feel mean and uncaring. People would rather say yes when you ask them. It is much easier for them to say yes if you are asking them to give you something you know they already have in excess. For some people you may not know what that is, but it usually doesn't take long to find out when you think about who you could ask.

Go back to the Treasure Map and start listing out the abundant resources of your board, staff, volunteers, etc. Take the time to look closely at each group or subgroup. You will notice that their resources may be different. For example, your board in general might have an abundance of passion, commitment, expertise, contacts, and money.

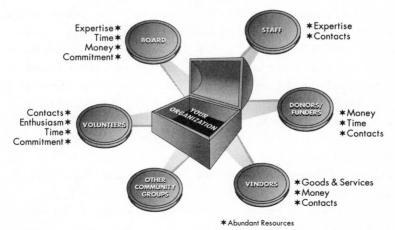

TREASURE MAP
ABUNDANT RESOURCES

* Abundant Resources

Yet your former board presidents may have additional resources, such as a long-term commitment to your organization or certain connections in the community.

Your volunteers might have an abundance of time, expertise, connections, and money as well. When you categorize volunteers by the type of program they are involved with, you will see more resources. Literacy tutors, for example, may have an abundance of teaching skill or an abundance of contacts in the educational field or an abundance of passion and personal stories to share from the people they have tutored.

How about your staff? They have an abundance of passion, firsthand stories about the good work of your organization, time (because they are being paid for their time at work), and expertise. Staff in different programs and departments will have different stories and different connections. Hospice nurses will have had direct contact with family members. Department directors may have more contact with the doctors. Take the time to do this with each group. What resources do they have in abundance?

Self-Interest

Next, go back over each group and ask what their self-interest would be in coming to your Point of Entry Event. What is the value or benefit for them in attending?

Let's pause a minute to talk about self-interest. Self-interest is a good thing. It drives everything we do. For example, you have a definite self-interest in reading this book. Maybe that self-interest is finding new ideas, maybe it is pleasing the boss, or maybe it is because you wanted a break from your work. Self-interest is always there, and as a person who is interested in raising funds, you should think of it as a very useful resource.

Self-interest can range from the most negative and selfish motives all the way to the most noble and inspiring. Consider the full range of self-interest as you go back to your Treasure Map and list the self-interests of each group.

Consider, for example, your donors or funders. What benefit does being connected to you have for them? Ask yourself, "What is

TREASURE MAP
SELF INTERESTS

Expertise ✱
Time ✱
Money ✱
Commitment ✱
Make a Difference ✪
Feel Good ✪
Personal Connection ✪
Please the Boss ✪

BOARD

STAFF

✱Expertise
✱Contacts
✪*Paycheck*
✪*Make a Difference*

Contacts ✱
Enthusiasm ✱
Time ✱
Commitment ✱
Make a Difference ✪
Contribute Talents ✪
Learn New Skills ✪
Socialize ✪

VOLUNTEERS

YOUR ORGANIZATION

DONORS/ FUNDERS

✱Money
✱Time
✱Contacts
✪*Tax Write-off*
✪*Feel Good*
✪*Make a Difference*

OTHER COMMUNITY GROUPS

VENDORS

✱Goods & Services
✱Money
✱Contacts
✪*Look Good to Others*
✪*They Really Care*
✪*New Business Contacts*

✱ Abundant Resources
✪ *Self-Interests*

in this for them?" Yes, they may want a tax write-off, but this is rarely the sole reason for making a gift. For most donors, a major self-interest is feeling good about making the gift and feeling they are making a difference. For some donors, self-interest is paying back someone for something they once received. Or maybe they have a personal connection to the services you offer. Or they feel that giving to your organization is a kind of insurance, that what you are committed to preventing won't happen to them. Guilt can be a self-interest, as well as impressing others and looking good. Maybe they are giving because they think it will help their child or grandchild to be accepted into your private school or college.

Look at the self-interest of your volunteers. Why are they involved with you? Perhaps it is to make a difference, to contribute their talents, to learn new skills, to build their resume for their next job, to give back, to feel important, to keep busy, and on and on. What about your board? For some, their self-interest is to please a boss who "asked" them to serve on your board. For others, it is a personal connection, a way of giving back, or a feel-good thing.

Donor for donor, self-interest is a key driver of your self-sustaining individual giving program. The sooner you know your donors' self-interest, whatever it may be, the easier it will be to customize your fundraising program to their needs. Down the road, as they become lifelong donors, you will want to think back to the self-interest that led to their involvement in the first place.

Fantasy Groups

Next, looking back at your Treasure Map, add in some fantasy categories. Who is not yet on your map that you would love to have associated with your organization? Whose involvement would leverage a whole world of support and credibility? Add those people to your Treasure Map, too. Some typical fantasy categories include celebrities, athletes, corporate executives, and media figures. For some

TREASURE MAP
FANTASY GROUP

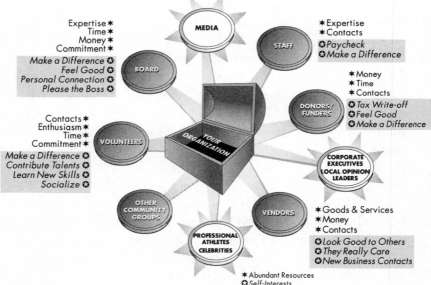

organizations, having the support of a local opinion leader, a religious leader, or an expert on your issue could quickly leverage your story into the larger community.

Let yourself play with this one. This is why it is fun to do a Treasure Map with a group of people.

Connecting the Groups

Finally, draw connecting lines between those groups on your Treasure Map who already talk to each other. You will see instantly how fast news travels. If a handful of people come to your sizzling Point of Entry Event, who else will they tell?

If your staff talks to your volunteers, draw a connecting line between those two groups. If your board and vendors talk only occasionally, you might draw a dotted line. For those groups who don't

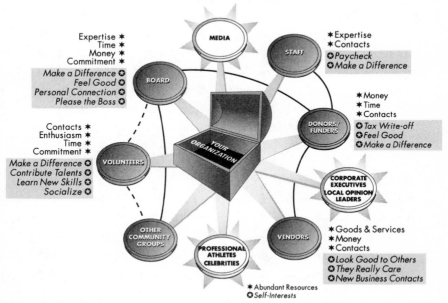

TREASURE MAP
WHO TALKS TO WHOM?

talk to each other at all, draw no connecting lines. Be sure to include your fantasy groups. Who on your organization's Treasure Map already might be talking with them? It is worth taking the time to go through this one category at a time. It can spark many insights.

Before moving on, stand back from your Treasure Map and notice which groups have the most lines connecting them to other groups. There may be so many lines leading to or from that group that it looks like a traffic jam. What does that tell you? These groups are key to leveraging others. They could naturally invite the people in these other groups to attend your Point of Entry Events because they are speaking to them all the time anyway.

A frequent example of a traffic-jam group is your staff. The staff is likely to be one group on the Treasure Map that talks to nearly every other group. What does that tell you? It should tell you that staff buy-in to your Point of Entry system is critical to your success. You will want to make a special effort to involve staff in the process. The easiest way to do this is to have special staff-only Point of Entry Events early on in the process. The staff can be invaluable in critiquing and refining the content at your Point of Entry. I remember how much we modified what we said at our school tours after taking the teachers through the tours and debriefing them individually about how to talk about the curriculum.

Conversely, if they have not fully bought into the process, the staff can be your biggest adversary. Go out of your way to let the staff know how essential their input is and how much you will need their support as you begin having regularly scheduled Point of Entry Events.

Personal Treasure Map

Next, give each team member a blank piece of paper and have them make a personal Treasure Map for themselves. Start by having people put their own names in the middle. Then have them go through the same steps of adding the groups they naturally come in contact with, what each group has in abundance, the self-interests of the groups in coming to a Point of Entry Event for your organization, their fantasy groups, and the lines connecting those who know each other. Give them enough time to get into doing the exercise. They probably will be surprised by all the treasure they have. Give them the time to go through all the steps.

Now, assuming your team has already attended a Point of Entry Event and knows what you are talking about, you can ask them to look back to their personal Treasure Maps and make a list of ten to twenty individuals they would feel comfortable inviting to a Point of Entry. Encourage them to have their list include people from each group on their Treasure Map, not just the "safest" groups of friends and family. Once they see the self-interest people have in coming to a Point of Entry, inviting them will become more of a game than a chore. They will realize that the person at the health club had already mentioned their interest in the environment or their mother's health problem. In other words, these people might actually want to come to learn more about your organization.

Some people on your team will have long, long lists of people they could invite. Do not make them feel awkward or embarrassed. There will naturally be people with more contacts than others. Long-time volunteers may have extensive lists of former volunteers they would like to invite. People in the health care profession may have more people on their personal Treasure Maps with self-interest in your health care work. Give everyone the time to make their lists or tell them to finish them after the meeting.

SAMPLE WORDING FOR INVITING GUESTS TO A POINT OF ENTRY

1. Hello, _____. You know how excited I am about the _____ organization.

2. I've been involved with them now for some time and I really feel we are changing the way people feel about _____. We've got a unique approach and a great new program for _____.

3. We are trying to get the word out into the community about our work and to get feedback about our programs and services.

4. I know you have talked with me before about your interest in solving this problem right here in our community.

5. _____ organization has begun offering a one-hour program and tour for people to see their work firsthand. I'd love to have you come and meet the real visionary who is the director and some of the great staff.

6. You won't be asked to make any financial contribution, but we would welcome your advice and feedback.

7. The dates and times of our next sessions/tours are _____.

ABOUT THE AUTHOR

Terry Axelrod is CEO and Founder of Benevon (formerly Raising More Money), which trains and coaches nonprofit organizations to implement a mission-based system for raising sustainable funding from individual donors. This system ends the suffering about fundraising and builds passionate and committed lifelong donors.

With nearly forty years of experience in the nonprofit field, Axelrod has founded three nonprofits in the fields of health care and affordable housing. She realized early in her career that the only path to sustainable funding was to systematically connect donors to the mission of the organization, then involve and cultivate them until they were clearly ready to give—in short, to treat donors the way you would treat a close friend or family member, someone with whom you planned to have a lifelong relationship.

Axelrod created the Benevon Model in 1996 after serving as Development Consultant to Zion Preparatory Academy, an inner-city Christian academy in Seattle, from 1992-1995. There she designed and implemented fundraising and marketing programs which yielded $7.2 million in two-and-a-half years as well as national recognition of the program, including a cover story in *The Chronicle of Philanthropy*.

Author of four books, *Raising More Money—A Step-by-Step Guide to Building Lifelong Donors, Raising More Money—The Point of Entry Handbook, Raising More Money—The Ask Event Handbook*, and *The Joy of Fundraising*, Axelrod is also a sought-after speaker, both nationally and internationally. Her passionate commitment to the possibility of sustainable funding for all nonprofits drives the mission of Benevon and each of its programs. "The donors are truly out there—wanting to contribute; it's up to the organizations to connect donors powerfully to their work and nurture that connection over time. Our programs give each organization the tools to do that successfully."

Terry currently serves as a Director of the Giving Institute, and Life Trustee of Swedish Medical Center. She received her Master's of Social Work and Bachelor's Degrees at the University of Michigan, and she resides in Seattle with her husband, Alan, and their two children.

ADDITIONAL INFORMATION
AND RESOURCES

Visit our Web site at www.benevon.com to:
- Subscribe to our free bi-weekly electronic newsletter, the Benevon E-New$.
- Register for one of our many free or inexpensive introductory sessions.
- Register for our Curriculum for Sustainable Funding.
- Purchase books and videos or DVDs about Benevon.
- Learn more about the Benevon Next-Step donor-tracking system.
- Browse the Benevon archives for additional information on building sustainable funding from lifelong individual donors.

INDEX